Brady,

Thanks again for

we are excited +

newest book. please

– Kyle Moore + Mark Woodland

Secrets of Top
Sales Performers

Compete Selling by SalesGym, LLC

41 East 400 North #138, Logan, UT 84321

Mark@salesgym.com

Editing: Glenn McMahan

Cover design: Andy Meaden and Ross Robinson

Text design: Andy Meaden

Print ISBN: 978-1-7320895-2-5

Ebook ISBN: 978-1-7320895-1-8

The definitive quick handbook on HOW to be more assertive on sales calls.

What readers are saying about *Compete Selling* ...

"How to be more assertive, and build relationships and trust at the same time."

"What every sales professional needs to know to sell in our modern, internet-driven world."

"Finally, a book on practical ideas and how to apply them immediately to increase sales."

"One of the clearest presentations of exactly what top performing salespeople do differently and how to apply their approaches to generate better results."

"I read this amazing book in one sitting. It's packed with great ideas and, more importantly, how to make those ideas work selling my services."

Opening Thoughts from the Authors ...

Getting better at sales is a lot like getting better at a sport. In sales, knowledge is not power until it is turned into skill, which we call verbal sales fluency. It takes the right ideas, practiced the right way, ideally with a strong practice coach to steadily improve. Top performing sales professionals are simply better at building trust, explaining their products and services in a compelling way, and being assertive in a way that opens up opportunity and doesn't come off as pushy or obnoxious.

Compete Selling is the first book we're aware of that actually shows sales professionals how to be more assertive in the right way, to blend the popular insight-challenger selling approaches with the more traditional consultative selling model that builds trust and credibility. Everyone says they want to be more assertive, but no one wants to be a jerk in the process. *Compete Selling* is a thorough guide to the best way to challenge, lead with insights, ask better, more provocative questions, and literally change the buying criteria of prospects and customers in a favorable way.

We (the authors of *Compete Selling*) have been working with sales teams for a combined one hundred years, having met and trained thousands of sales professionals from most of the Fortune 500 companies over the years. We've also worked with small and mid-sized companies, and one thing we've learned, for certain, when it comes to helping salespeople improve sales, there are several bad habits that get in the way their success:

- Talking too much on sales calls and not listening enough
- Not asking the right questions to open up the right sales conversation
- Talking about their products/services in a way that doesn't have maximum impact
- Not talking to enough prospects and customers that have the authority to make big purchasing decisions
- Lacking the ability to be assertive in the right way that opens up new thinking and opportunity on sales calls
- Poor verbal skills when it comes to communicating their value proposition and, competitive advantages and an inability to use that information throughout the sales process

We started the SalesGym in 2016 to test and refine a much more effective way to break those bad habits and build the skills and habits of top performers. Day after day, we listen to our clients' top performers, paying close attention to how they interact with prospects and customers. Then, we teach the rest of the team to learn and apply those approaches. *Compete Selling* is a direct outcome of all those thousands of hours over the years spent studying the gap between top performers and everyone else.

Compete Selling contains a simple and distilled version of everything we've learned along the way. It all starts with MASTERING the sales messaging that will give you the ingredients to build more sales with. This book will show you why top performers communicate differently and how you can use their approaches. You'll learn how to ask better questions, when and how to be more assertive, and how to close for bigger outcomes.

We have also built a companion learning system on competeselling.com for you to use to go deeper into the practice system to get better at selling.

Thank you for your interest in *Compete Selling* and we look forward to hearing from you!

Contents

One

Compete Selling Overview

Effective selling is an art and a science. Numbers matter in terms of seeing enough of the right people who lead to more sales. This includes closing ratios, market share, and a gazillion other data points that are tracked in complex pipeline reporting systems all adding up to the numbers game. There are many good books about the science and technology components of selling, and we want to say right up front . . . THAT STUFF IS IMPORTANT.

But that's *not* what this book is about. This book is about what assertive, top performing sales professionals say and do when speaking to a prospect, customer, client, or referral source to generate maximum impact and results. *Compete Selling* is about HOW to be more assertive in sales calls while building trust and influence at a deeper, more impactful level. The book is also about HOW to develop these skills with all the resources you need and a system of practice that will enable you to improve.

Although there are many factors that influence sales results, most sales professionals agree that it comes down to six standout elements:

1. Seeing the right people who can buy a lot of what you sell (activity level)
2. Verbal command of sales messaging including: competitive advantages, differentiating factors, and the value proposition; ability to deliver a powerful message under pressure with confidence and credibility
3. Being skillful at an effective and (when necessary) assertive sales process that works for your business
4. Learning and improving through steady, rigorous practice
5. Utilizing technology, social platforms, communications, and presentation tools to positively amplify your results
6. Discipline, self motivation, and drive to succeed

Compete Selling is a real-world improvement system designed to help you develop a more assertive and effective approach to sales calls so that you can generate better, faster sales results. *Compete Selling* is based on the remarkably effective way that highly skilled athletes improve. So, hopefully this book will give you a motivational burst as well.

Better techniques + better practice + better coaching = better results

Professional athletes train and practice every week to get better. The difference between the top golfer on the PGA Tour and all the rest is usually less than one stroke per round, but it takes a lot of practice to get that one stroke advantage. The fastest sprinter on the planet is a fraction of a second faster than the next ten behind him. The same is true in sales; a small advantage over your competitors will give you a huge boost in results. *Compete Selling* provides a powerful way for you to get better results by becoming more confident and assertive when it's needed, and more effective at all aspects of the sales process.

Prior to the economic crisis in 2008-2009, virtually all professional sales teams were trained in one version or another of consultative selling. There were many names for it, with different authors and training groups proclaiming a new and better version; but, for the most part, they boiled down to the same underlying components:

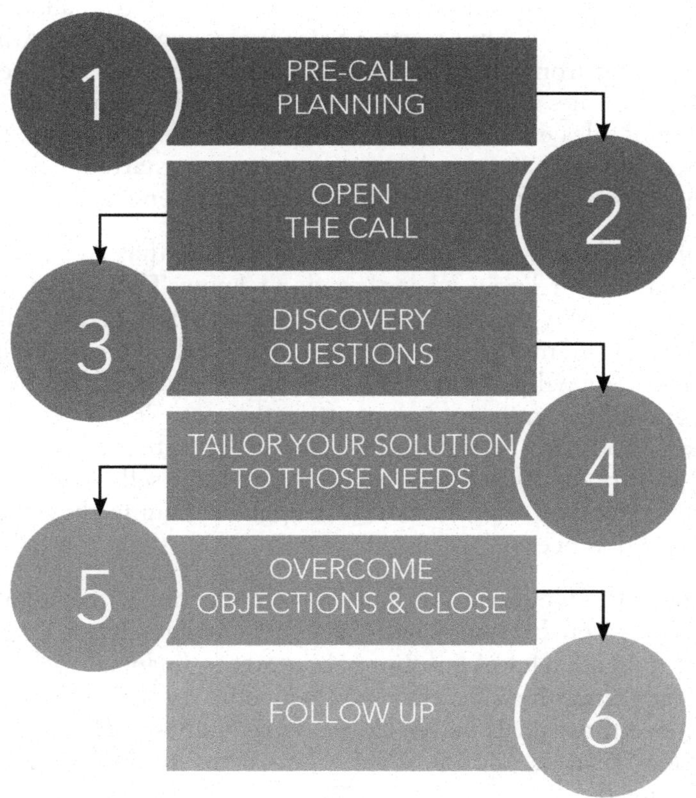

Some of these approaches emphasized complex, multi-influencer strategies, focusing on long-cycle, enterprise selling, and some emphasized a transactional or short-term focus. The general idea was to plan your call, build trust and rapport, ask a lot of good discovery questions, and then tailor a solution that felt "just right" based on what you learned from the prospect. Doing this was seen as a way of minimizing resistance and objections. (From this point forward, we will refer to prospects, clients, customers, referral sources, and influencers as "PCCRs," to cover all the bases.)

After the 2008-2009 economic shock, a game changing book called *The Challenger Sale* was published. It presented research on why certain types of salespeople generate consistently better results. Extensive research indicated that relationship-focused salespeople using consultative selling were not getting the best results . . . not even close. The salespeople who were leading the way used an assertive and provocative approach called "challenger selling." We prefer the term "Highly Assertive Sales Professionals" or "HASPs." (We'll use that acronym from this point forward when referring to these assertive, more successful sales professionals.) That book had a significant impact on the thinking of sales executives and managers all over the world. Every year since it was published, more and more sales managers started looking for ways to get their salespeople to be more assertive and challenging during sales calls.

The premise underlying this assertive selling style is that, in many cases, the PCCRs simply don't know what they don't know. They often use buying criteria that are likely to cause a poor buying decision. HASP selling is less product focused and more focused on changing the thinking or buying criteria first. Those criteria will line-up better with the products and services thereby giving salespeople a significant competitive advantage. It's not just about who has the best products and services; it's about the right way to *evaluate and choose* the best products and services. In consultative selling, we assume that PCCRs understand all that. In HASP selling, we assume they don't, and it makes a big difference.

An example of this would be a financial advisor meeting with a high-networth PCCR who is reasonably happy with his or her current advisor. A consultative approach would ask a lot of questions about needs, financial goals, retirement plans, college savings for kids, etc., and then come up with a plan to help the PCCR achieve those goals better than a current advisor. However, it's likely that the "new" plan or solution will be similar to the PCCR's current plan. That's because the PCCR has probably given the same information to the consultative seller, including the exact same needs and concerns he gave the current advisor.

The HASP approach would be different. Instead of asking questions only about the investor's financial needs and goals, this salesperson would look for the thinking behind the financial plan and the investor's unwitting mistakes. The HASP might make the investor aware of the unnecessary risks of the current investment approach, such as the big mistake of not using a more creative approach to trusts and tax strategies. Once the HASP gets the PCCR to doubt the current advisor's advice and plan, he has created a big advantage. He has essentially CHANGED THE THINKING and decision-making criteria of the investor in his favor before presenting a product or solution.

Another example is a salesperson who sells digital advertising services. He is meeting with an owner of seven high-end restaurants who has decided to take a look at several advertising agencies for her upcoming year's marketing strategy. A consultative seller would come in and find out she wants to spend the bulk of her budget on radio, TV, and print, just as she's done for the last twenty years. The restaurant owner just wants better results. So the consultative seller listens to her strategy and then comes up with similar plans on how to execute her objectives, focusing on her long-held beliefs that TV and radio advertising is the best strategy.

The HASP would spend more time understanding why the restaurant owner wants to spend 90 percent of her budget on radio, TV, and print, and then challenge the validity of that marketing approach. Instead, he offers insight into the explosive results, measurements, and flexibility that is possible if the restaurant owner would allocate more of her budget to digital media and, in particular, mobile, which is barely on her radar. He shows the owner how mobile can reach big-spending tourists and business travelers in a way that traditional advertising can't. More importantly, he explains why changing her thinking about her advertising budget will help her reach her goal of opening three more restaurants. The owner's decision-making criteria are rocked by this interaction. She rethinks her basic assumptions and realizes that her strategy is not keeping up with the trends. Just as important, she becomes annoyed that her current agency has not made her aware of these trends. Our HASP now has an advantage over his competitors because he has provided a proposal that expands the restaurant owner's digital advertising allocation with a bigger emphasis on mobile to bring in new customers that can't be reached with her old marketing strategy.

A third example would be Food Dimensions, a company that manages food and cafeteria services for large corporate clients. The HASP gets an appointment with the person in a large bank that makes the decisions about which company manages the food services on the bank's corporate campus for six thousand employees. Instead of asking questions about cost and efficiency (the current provider's forte), he asks questions about how the bank is recruiting and attracting top tech talent. He shows the decision-maker how critical food services can be in the strategy to attract this talent. He describes how the cafeteria and coffee stations around the buildings are an essential strategic recruiting and employee retention investment. This gives the decision-maker a whole new vision of how food services could be more strategically positioned at the bank.

The HASP also compares the budget of the bank to leading tech companies, and he makes the case that it is woefully inadequate in the ultra-competitive war to attract top tech talent. Using videos, he shows the decision-maker how Food Dimensions has served high-profile companies with a food service strategy that brings employees together and encourages more collaboration and innovation. After arranging for the decision-maker to visit a Food Dimensions client, a tech company, the HASP points out how ordinary and uninteresting the bank's current menu and overall cafeteria design is, and how this problem is hurting the bank's recruiting strategy. The HASP criticizes the bank's current food strategy, but he does it in a helpful way. It turns out to be a game changing insight for the buyer who then makes a decision to change the bank's strategy in a way that lines up better with Food Dimension's competitive advantages and weakens the position of Food Dimension's competitor. This allows his proposal, which comes in at a whopping 28 percent HIGHER than the current supplier's fees, to be more desirable because cost is no longer the main issue.

The consultative selling approach would have been to focus on what was important to the decision-maker. That approach would make a sale nearly impossible, because the bank's current provider was the well established low cost and efficiency leader. As long as the decision-maker's focus was on cost and efficiency, the Food Dimensions salesperson was at a severe disadvantage.

A final example would be of a small upstart CRM company going up against the industry standard behemoths that have most of the market share. Instead of asking questions about needs, features, reporting, and other capabilities that the salesperson knows she doesn't have an advantage in, the HASP instead asks questions about how well the company utilizes its current CRM system. She surveys the sales and customer service teams to determine their attitudes and adoption of the current system and its capabilities. She presents survey after survey of employees in the industry who utilize less than 20 percent of the features they're paying for. She also demonstrates the yearly cost of all that underutilization. Then, she presents clear information and research on how personalized training and support is more important than a ridiculously complex set of features that no one uses. This helps the decision-maker to realize how poorly the company utilizes its current system. As the HASP emphasizes ease of use, customized training, and a long-term adoption strategy, she demonstrates the strength and competitive advantage of her much smaller upstart company. She has changed the thinking of the decision-maker in her favor.

The HASP method is about challenging the thinking of PCCRs with more assertive questions, ideas, and insights that are contrary to conventional thinking. This approach involves an interaction style that shakes the PCCR out of typical decision-making models or paradigms in a positive way. It's more assertive, provocative, and risky because it can fracture trust if not done skillfully.

It's important to understand that *The Challenger Sale* did not invent a new sales process; the authors simply observed and documented a selling approach that top performers have been using for years. Likewise, the founders of the SalesGym have worked with hundreds of sales teams from top companies and we have identified some surprising misconceptions when it comes to consultative selling and insight-led, assertive selling. We've met many HASPs that are far bolder and assertive during sales calls. Some have produced better results and some haven't.

What *The Challenger Sale* didn't really report was that the same assertive approaches that top HASP performers use can also alienate PCCRs if the approach is not done skillfully. In other words, there are many poor performers that use assertive HASP methods with less skill and get terrible results. Top performers are better when it comes to interpersonal skills, consultative selling skills, and communicating the essential sales messaging of their value propositions, competitive advantages, and differentiating factors. Without these critical skills, HASP methods can feel aggressive and pushy. This is critical to understand. More often than not, the highly assertive salespeople that generate the best results are also FANTASTIC at consultative selling. So, in the challenger model, the "challenger" type of top performer is also a relationship builder. Assertive selling approaches require better interpersonal, sales messaging, and consultative skills.

Compete Selling is about developing a success accelerating set of skills that is built and reinforced with steady practice.

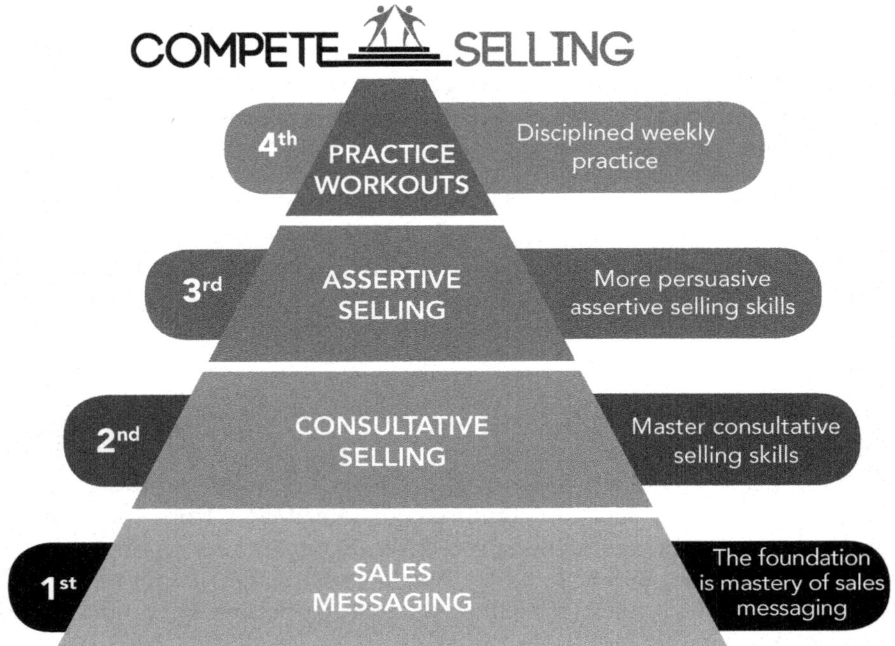

This graphic illustrates that the foundation of effective selling is the mastery of persuasive and concise verbal sales messaging around your value proposition, competitive advantages, and differentiating factors. Then you need to be good at consultative selling skills that build relationships. These skills will allow you to learn and use the more assertive selling approaches that the best HASPs use. Finally, you need a practice system for steady, weekly practice, just like top athletes.

Compete Selling is about the integration of consultative selling and the more assertive HASP approaches, and the book shows you exactly how to do it. It is the complete package of what you need to master to become a top performer.

- Mastery of sales messaging
- Mastery of consultative selling
- Mastery of more assertive, HASP approaches that challenge and change the thinking of PCCRs
- HOW to practice, improve, and gain a big advantage on your competitors the same way elite athletes do it

We're going to go deeper into all four of these areas so you can learn what top performers are doing, and more importantly, learn step-by-step how to do it yourself. Given the size and scope of this topic, this book could easily stretch to more than five hundred pages, but we're not going to ask you to go through that kind of torture. We're going to keep it short, concise, and easy to get through quickly. This book is your ticket to more information and details available at our website, competeselling.com. The book and website were developed together to give you the absolute best learning experience possible. We have audio and video examples and demonstrations of these approaches in an interactive format that will help you develop skills that a book simply can't give you. Competeselling.com will have training guides, practice tools, and worksheets, and the SalesGym has the highly trained practice coaches that can give you the same training advantage elite athletes have.

If you'd like more information on the team that put this book together, our backgrounds are on competeselling.com. We're all lifelong salespeople who have started and built sales training consulting companies. We train and coach sales teams everyday in the SalesGym and have been doing this for over twenty-five years with small and medium-size companies. We also work with many of the largest, most recognizable companies in the world, such as Google, American Funds, Electronic Arts, Capital Group, BlackRock, Facebook, Anthem, and PIMCO.

This book is written in my (Michael St. Lawrence) voice to give it a coherent narrative, but the ideas come from all of us. You'll find helpful "pro-tips" throughout the book from our founding team at the SalesGym.

We founded the SalesGym in 2016 as a place where sales teams can practice with highly skilled practice coaches (similar to personal trainers in a gym, for instance) that help them break bad habits and learn how to use consultative selling along with more assertive *Compete Selling* approaches to generate maximum results. Our team has, collectively, more than one hundred years of experience working with thousands of salespeople from all over the world. We've created a better, more effective way to sell, and more importantly, a better way to practice and train the same way elite athletes do.

We see a massive gap between salespeople who understand the concepts (most do) and salespeople who communicate their message with fluency, confidence, and conviction every time, when the money is on the line (most don't). The SalesGym was created to close that gap and help more salespeople win more often. Top athletes don't practice for two or three days a couple times a year and expect to perform well in competition. Amazingly, a lot of salespeople go to occasional sales seminars, maybe once or twice a year and then spend little time practicing to get better. Athletes go to the gym and the practice field frequently, and so do top salespeople.

Because we practice with sales teams every day in the SalesGym, our experience is very practical and not academic. We're in the trenches with real salespeople and sales managers preparing for sales calls happening today and tomorrow. We know your challenges, the reality of how competitive it is and how important it is to master the fundamentals in this book. We bring them to you with enthusiasm and the assurance that they can be a springboard for you to become a top performer in every possible definition of the word!

Two

The Compete Selling Sales Process

The Compete Sales Process integrates consultative selling with more assertive HASP elements needed to challenge the thinking of PCCRs that often don't realize their thinking is causing poor decisions. *Compete Selling* reduces the risks of overly aggressive and pushy sales approaches that can fracture trust and rapport.

Although there are a number of different consultative models out there, let's take another quick look at the most fundamental stripped-down version:

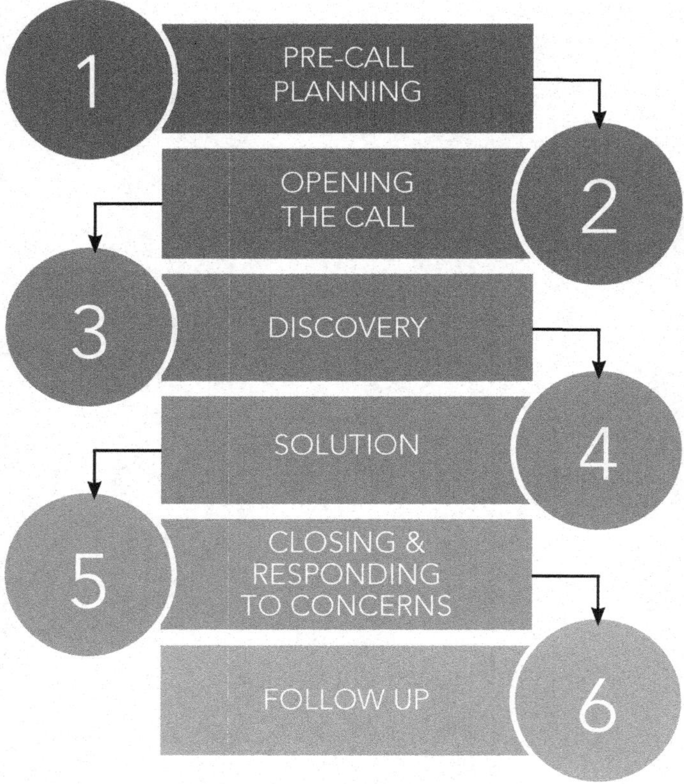

There are more processes within each of these steps, but these are the essentials. Pre-call planning and follow-up occur before and after the call, and the four steps in the middle happen in the sales call itself. Even short prospecting calls to generate interest and an appointment for a longer interaction follow a similar process. Although this book is not geared toward prospecting (that's a big topic), the short, effective sales messaging that we'll cover in the next chapter is a major piece of prospecting for new business. Let's take a quick look at each of the six steps of the consultative sales process.

Pre-Call Planning

This is the planning needed to get ready for the call, including identifying the goals and desired outcomes, developing the agenda, and establishing the questions and possible key points to emphasize. This step also includes researching the company and the PCCR, and rehearsing to get ready for the call. We often need to review the notes from the last meeting in order to summarize where we are. It's also helpful to review personal information, such as names of kids, where the PCCR went to college, etc., to have details fresh in our mind for rapport building purposes.

Opening the Call

Opening the call has to do with the preliminary pleasantries, transitioning to an effective agenda, gaining agreement on the agenda, and anything we do before we start asking questions or presenting a solution. This can mean introductions of people in the meeting, a recap of our last meeting, and a brief company overview, if needed.

Discovery / Questions

Generally, after we open the call, we either ask discovery questions or, if we've already finished that step and are returning with a solution presentation, we'll do a quick recap of needs to get into the flow of our last meeting. Ideally, discovery includes asking interesting and relevant questions that increase understanding of the PCCR's needs, thinking, and decision-making influences while building rapport and lowering resistance.

Solution Presentation

After we've completed the discovery step and confirmed our understanding of the PCCR's needs, we must respond with a product/service presentation or solution. This is where we tailor our proposed ideas in a way that is hopefully appealing. Consultative selling is designed to reduce concerns and objections by tailoring the solution so well that the PCCR is excited about it. In many cases, however, it doesn't work out that way; the PCCR often has questions and/or concerns, which is when the friction in the interaction generally increases.

Responding to Concerns / Gaining Commitment

In this step, we identify what concerns the PCCR may have and then respond to them. This step is similar to the entire sales process. We typically ask more questions, continue to tailor a solution, and then recommend an action step to test for commitment. Depending on the product and length of the sales cycle, the commitment we seek might be an actual order or a step toward an order. Either way, we need something for the PCCR to say yes to at this stage. We need to move the ball forward.

Follow-Up

This is everything that happens after the call to keep commitments or promises, and to provide additional information and decision influencing evidence to keep the process moving. In longer sales cycles, follow-up, including summaries and recaps, is a key part of making sure action steps and recommendations get done.

That was roughly five hundred words to describe a very complex interaction that literally thousands of pages have been written about. There is much more to it, obviously, and we're going to go into more depth in this book, too; but from an overview perspective, that's how consultative selling works. Virtually every consultative selling model out there is built on this simple interactive approach.

This process is diagnostic in nature, similar to what we hopefully experience when we go to a physician to seek a cure for an illness. Ideally, the doctors we see spend a moment helping us get comfortable and relaxed. Then they preview what they're going to do, then they ask questions and do tests to diagnose the problem, then they propose a way to cure or fix the problem. Finally, they get us to commit to their recommendation and we decide together what the next step is. That is exactly what the consultative process is all about.

Consultative selling works very well . . . until it doesn't. There are some specific reasons why consultative selling doesn't always work as effectively as it used to.

- Often, the PCCR is very comfortable with the current supplier or provider, and the hassle and risk of switching for what they may see as minimal benefit isn't worth it to them.
- Sometimes, the PCCR is stuck in a way of thinking that prevents them from seeing the value of a new service. This is often the case when a

product or service is new and innovative. The explosion of options and innovations is one of the reasons why consultative sellers aren't generating the good results they used to produce.

- Since 2009, there has been a sharp decrease in trust of institutions. The Internet has made us increasingly skeptical of claims, facts, and evidence. Simultaneously, it is much easier for PCCRs to research the companies they do business with, and they are a lot less patient in the buying process. They expect salespeople to get to the point quicker with less time wasted in the often lengthy discovery step of consultative selling.
- Consultative selling works better when the PCCR is honest. Because everyone is bombarded with advertising and sales calls, a lot of PCCRs are skillful at hiding their needs if they feel it is in their best interest to do so.
- PCCRs will often hide their most important objection because they are uncomfortable bringing it up. Or they hold back as part of a negotiating tactic.
- Consultative selling works best when the PCCR knows what they need and no one else is filling that need. In these cases, it's a perfect fit. When the PCCR doesn't know his or her needs, however, consultative selling is a mismatch.
- Consultative selling is, to a large extent, about building trust and rapport, and lowering resistance. When the PCCR puts out an objection or says something like, "I need some time to think about it," it's often too late to save the sale. PCCRs often make their decisions early in the sales process. Typically, sales pressure comes at the end of the process and PCCRs know how to avoid it.

Our insights from years of studying and working with HASPs, reveal that being more assertive in the discovery/questioning step and presenting more contrarian ideas and insights earlier in the process, well before the solution, will have a better impact on the buyer's decision-making criteria.The sales messaging of HASPs is much more dynamic and persuasive. HASPs know when and how to use messaging that is more provocative and, at times, edgy. There are lots of suggestions in the books that present research about how HASPs operate, but in terms of how to apply and adapt the HASP approach to specific products and services, the books don't offer much.

That's Where Compete Selling Comes In!

Compete Selling demonstrates how to BLEND consultative and more assertive HASP selling to get better results.

Now we'll take a look at the strengths of consultative and assertive HASP selling, then at the risks and weaknesses of each approach, and finally at the approach that takes the best of both—*Compete Selling*.

Strengths of Consultative and "HASP" Approaches

Consultative Selling Strengths	Assertive HASP Selling Strengths
The focus is always on building the relationship, strengthening trust, and understanding the customer to tailor a solution based on what they want.	EXTREME verbal mastery of sales messaging, including the value proposition, competitive advantages, and differentiating factors. It all starts here.
The agenda is usually focused on what's most important to the PCCR and, in some cases, the PCCR actually sets the agenda.	In pre-call planning, HASPs determine bold (stretch) and fallback outcomes, and they commit to going after them, regardless of the risk.
A primary objective of consultative selling is to reduce resistance and increase receptivity through a comfortable and rapport building interaction.	The agenda is far more assertive and focused on PCCR biases or beliefs to challenge and change the thinking of the PCCR.
When asked effectively, questions identify exactly what the customer wants, why they want it, and what the solution should be to make the sale.	HASPs intentionally bring up uncomfortable topics that expose erroneous thinking and buying criteria that might cause a bad buying decision.
Trust is built by listening to what matters most to the PCCR and showing that we are focused on those needs.	More provocative questions are carefully thought out and prepared so they can be asked in a way to shake the PCCR out of current thinking.
The solution is built around the prospect's interests, and we use the PCCR's language to explain how our products/services and solutions will solve the PCCR'S problems.	Extreme attention is given to bring in the thinking of other customers that value a different set of buying criteria that generates better results. This is done through skillful use of customer-oriented phrasing.

Ideally, objections and concerns are minimized because the proposed solution is such a good fit.	Likely objections are moved up in the sales process and identified as early as possible so they are addressed before closing or next-step recommendations are made.
Objections are identified, usually after the solution, with questions, listening, and more tailored solutions to overcome them.	Powerful insights and evidence are presented to amplify the risks of a poor decision based on the buying criteria used by the PCCR.
Commitments and next steps are identified and followed-up consistently to continue to build trust.	Recommendations that are easy for a PCCR to accept are prepared in hopes of moving the sales process forward. Every sales call ends with an assertive ask or recommendation.

Each of these approaches have serious weaknesses or risks. Consultative selling is most effective when you have strong rapport and the PCCR trusts you enough to provide honest answers to your questions. This, however, is often NOT the case. Salespeople who give higher priority to building relationships are often uncomfortable asking assertive questions because they don't want to risk damaging rapport. As a result, they often don't discover the resistance factors until it's too late. Finally, if the PCCR only provides limited information, then the salesperson has a reduced ability to talk about big-picture solutions. This locks the salesperson into a more transactional, product-and-service focus, which leaves the bigger opportunity on the table for the competitors. Finally, consultative salespeople who emphasize relationship building are often hesitant to ask for the order when they feel significant resistance is likely from the PCCR.

On the other hand, when a salesperson attempts to use assertive approaches without the skill and experience needed to do it the right way, he or she could run even bigger risks, including:

- The PCCR could become frustrated and reject the salesperson, regardless of how good the ideas, products, or services might be.
- Assertive questions can backfire if they're not set up the right way. The PCCR can shut down and/or give dishonest answers to end the dialogue as quickly as possible.

- If the salesperson does not have strong sales messaging and ability with the consultative sales process, he or she will fail when using more assertive sales approaches.
- HASPs must have objective and credible high-impact insights and evidence to back up new ideas about buying criteria. And if that evidence is too self-serving, the whole process will backfire.
- Assertiveness, if it's not used skillfully, can easily be experienced by the PCCR as deal-killing obnoxious pressure.
- Once salespeople lose rapport and trust with a client, it's nearly impossible to rebuild it, especially with someone we're not yet doing business with.

PRO TIP from Emily Knott:

> *What really distinguishes* Compete Selling *is the fluency, or mastery, of sales messaging as a high priority along with learning how and when to apply assertive techniques to the consultative model. Most salespeople are fairly effective at following a process, especially when one has been outlined for them and most likely sits on their desk in some form of a laminated job aid. What is more difficult to master is the skill of actually verbalizing each step of a sales process with real confidence under pressure. Compete Selling teaches you how to effectively communicate in each step of the process, starting with mastering your competitive advantages and learning how to be appropriately assertive. Compete Selling guides you in winning more sales.*

By the time you finish this book, you'll understand how to blend both consultative and assertive selling approaches to generate the best possible results. At the risk of being repetitive, we need to be great at both consultative and assertive selling approaches. *Compete Selling* demonstrates how to do this. This graphic gives some detail about how consultative and HASP selling approaches are blended to create the *Compete Selling* approach.

Consultative Selling Elements	Stage	Assertive Selling Elements
• Understand background of PCCR • Pre-call planning checklist is used • Careful review of previous interactions	1 PRE-CALL PLANNING	• Develop assertive stretch outcomes and goals • Identify biases and likely objections to focus on • Mastery of sales messaging before the call
• Build rapprt early • PCCR-oriented agenda • PCCR's agenda priorities are included	2 OPENING THE CALL	• Agenda built to introduce new thinking • Value driven messaging • Biases and concerns brought into the agenda
• Trust building questioning flow is used • Strong listening & trust building focus • Strong summary to focus on PCCR's needs	3 DISCOVERY 2.0	• More assertive questions are used • Positioning used to soften assertive questions • Concerns & buying criteria often challenged
• Summary driven features and benefits • Continuous reinforcement of buyer's needs • Focus on using same terms as PCCR • Solution Presentation / demo • Test for interest throughout	4 PARADIGM BUSTING SOLUTIONS	• HASP focus on sales headlines • Better customer-oriented phrasing throughout • Evidence is brought in • Assertive use of objection vaccinations • Focus on risk of not changing
• Focus on identifying & overcoming concerns • Questions & evidence used to resolve concerns • Next step recommendations used and re-used	5 GAINING COMMITMENT	• Stretch and fallback outcomes carefully set up • Success stories used to set up closing process • Expose hidden risks of not changing or using outdated buying criteria • Makes it easy to say yes to commitment
• Review of commitments • Clarify next steps • Build trust by keeping commitments	6 FOLLOW UP	• Tie down details & next steps in writing • Continue to bring new ideas that influence buying criteria

Compete Selling is the way to be more assertive on sales calls without fracturing rapport and trust. It's great to say, "Hey, you need to be more assertive and aggressive on sales calls," until you make a PCCR angry because you didn't do it in an effective way. *Compete Selling* is the "how to win friends and influence people" approach to assertive selling. We'll show you exactly where in the consultative process the assertive elements can be added, and how to apply them in a way that improves rapport and trust, which is the secret of the top-performers. These approaches will challenge thinking and build greater trust, simultaneously.

The Elements of Compete Selling

Consultative selling continues to be the framework or basic flow of interaction. That's because it's the best process for influence. Here are some adjustments we make when we want to be more pleasantly assertive.

- Our sales messaging about our value proposition, competitive advantages, and differentiating factors has a stronger impact on sales interaction.
- We use a better approach to setting up provocative questions in a way that doesn't destroy rapport.
- We introduce the thinking of other people that contrasts with the PCCR's thinking or buying criteria in a way that is helpful to the PCCR.
- We use customer-oriented phrasing in a way that makes it much easier for the PCCR to see better ways of thinking and better buying criteria that will produce better outcomes.
- We understand how the process fits together to generate bolder outcomes, which we plan for in advance and which leads the sales interaction forward.

It's not just what we do, but HOW we do it. This is especially true when it comes to assertive and provocative selling approaches. We need to remember that HASPs can create better or worse results depending on how they apply their assertiveness.

We're going to look at each step of the consultative process more closely, and at how we can use the *Compete Selling* elements in a skillful way that will move the ball forward quicker, especially with resistant PCCRs. We'll give you all the tools and practice exercises to get better fast. One of our SalesGym founders, Mark Woodland, explains how balancing emotional and logical needs is so important.

PRO TIP from Mark Woodland

> *Have you ever heard a prospect say, "I understand exactly what you're saying….It makes total sense, but I think we're going to hold off for now." Or worse yet, they smile and nod and give you the impression they are onboard…but you never hear from them again. Chances are you logically made your point, but emotionally they never "bought into" your product/service. There is an old adage that I love: logic drives conclusion, emotion drives action. If you want your prospects to say yes, you have to move beyond logic (data, charts, features) and help them feel and imagine success (benefits, opportunity, possibilities, problems solved, etc.). That's what Compete Selling is all about..*

As Mark points out, we need to be good at both the logical and emotional elements of the sales process. *Compete Selling* is the best process to blend the two for better results.

Three

Sales Messaging

You will not reach your potential as a sales professional if you do not master your sales messaging. Please re-read that first sentence at least three times until it really sinks in. It doesn't matter if you are a master of consultative selling and assertive HASP approaches if you can't answer these six questions in a k*nock it out of the park* kinda way:

- Who are you? What do you do? Why does it matter?
- What makes your products and services better or different than your competitors?
- Why should I meet with you when I'm happy with my current supplier/provider?
- What can you give me that I'm not already getting?
- What is your company's value proposition in ninety seconds or less?
- What big, game changing, and disruptive ideas can you introduce to the conversation?

"Sales messaging" is what we use to answer these important questions, which nearly every PCCR has before they'll do business with you. The best sales messaging is concise and interesting. It creates an immediate "tell me more" response because it generates curiosity and lowers resistance. As you can see, the foundation of our *Compete Selling* model and logo is sales messaging; it's that important.

We have spent thousands of hours working with salespeople, experienced and inexperienced, over the last twenty-five years. It is shocking how many experienced and assertive salespeople cannot quickly and persuasively explain their value proposition. Some call this the sixty-second elevator pitch, but it's much more than that. To master sales messaging you must know:

- Your company's value proposition
- Your competitive advantages and differentiating factors that make your products, services, and solutions different and better
- How to say, in sixty seconds or less, why a PCCR should meet with or speak with you for the first time
- How to introduce yourself in a meeting the right way
- The extremely powerful three-by-three presentation method to cement your competitive advantages in the minds of the people you meet with
- Disruptive insights that impact buying criteria and underlying buying assumptions
- Several success stories of customers who are benefitting in important ways from your products, services, and solutions
- The critical factors with which you can "vaccinate" your competition

Think of sales messaging as the INGREDIENTS you have to work with. A master chef may have the most effective cooking techniques on the planet, but if she doesn't have the best ingredients, it really doesn't matter. If she starts a marinara sauce with poor quality tomatoes, the sauce is going to suffer no matter how she tries to improve it. If the shrimp in her scampi dish are not fresh, the end product will not be as good. Your sales messaging is, essentially, your selling ingredients. If you don't have great messaging, your sales process is not going to work even if you can communicate with confidence under pressure. We first need to get the basics of our messaging down in a simple way, then we need to learn how to tailor it to specific selling situations.

Before we begin most training projects, we test our new clients' sales teams on their sales messaging skill level. We do this even in the largest companies that spend a significant amount on sales training. Here are the mistakes we find most often:

- Too much inside jargon and use of terms that don't mean much to a decision-maker
- Filled with meaningless buzzwords
- Rushed with nothing notable or memorable
- Too generic, sounding too similar to the competitor(s)

- Slow moving and repetitive
- No emotional punch

To illustrate, compare the following hypothetical answer to a simple question: "What sets you apart from your competitors?"

> We are the industry's leading provider of digital advertising solutions and insights. We help our customers reach more of their target markets more efficiently than they've ever done before. We combine state of the art, cutting edge digital analytics with our ability to understand our customer's needs and strategy. It's our ability to put together a more cost-effective strategy to reach more of our clients' target markets that distinguishes us from our competitors. Our integrated approach of combining a comprehensive digital and traditional advertising strategy is what sets us apart.

Compare that example to this more customer friendly one:

> That's a great question. It's on the mind of nearly everyone we talk to these days. What our customers prefer about our approach is that we work closely with them to get a deeper understanding of their target market and what makes those customers tick. We use our digital analytics to study consumer buying habits. Working together with our clients, we learn the best way to interact with those consumers to drive more of the right traffic, which results in more profitable sales. Our customers tell us they like how we don't just focus on hitting a huge market with expensive repeated impressions, but that we get to their target customers with engaging messaging and content that draws them into a richer, more enjoyable, relevant buying experience. Our customers tell us we've helped them transform their marketing strategy because we focus on conversion of leads into sales and not just clicks and views. One of my customers summed it up well when he told me that while other agencies focus on marketing strategy, allocation, and spend, we focus on engaging our clients' consumers and prospective consumers in a way that helps them buy more, when they're looking. So, I'm curious, how are you integrating your value proposition message and content to draw your customers into an engaging buying experience?

There are more examples to review on competeselling.com.

If you're like most PCCRs, you'll respond much better to the second example. Let's examine why:

1. We use lots of customer-oriented phrasing.
2. We focus on what's important to a customer, not on what's important to us
3. We communicate outcomes and benefits from the customer's perspective which is more interesting for the customer.
4. We reduce the internal buzzwords and jargon and use language that is more relevant to the customer's interests.

We're going to talk a lot in this book about customer-oriented thinking, phrasing, and communication. It's a core fundamental of the *Compete Selling* approach. If you are going to be more assertive, you have to learn how to say things in a way that doesn't bore or alienate the listener. That's what customer-oriented phrasing can do for you.

To achieve mastery at sales messaging, a good place to start is to learn and practice the CPET technique to answering questions. Nearly every sales interaction is going to involve questions from the PCCR, so this is a very practical technique. Here's what the acronym CPET stands for:

C = Cushion

P = Prompters into customer-oriented phrasing

E = Explain the details

T = Transition to an open-ended question

A cushion is a simple phrase to begin responding to a question. For instance, if a custom home builder was asked, "Can you tell me a little about how you handle changes and upgrades from the original estimate?" a cushion would be, "That's a great question and I'm glad you asked."

We use cushions to show the PCCR we WELCOME questions and concerns. We assure them that we aren't defensive or annoyed by them. This helps lower resistance and takes some of the friction and pressure out of the interaction. Cushions should not be formulaic; they should be conversational. Here's several examples (there are many more on competeselling.com).

- That's an interesting question that's on the mind of a lot of customers we work with.
- I really appreciate you asking me that; it shows me you're focused on the right things.
- That's a question I've been getting a lot recently and I appreciate you're asking it.
- I'm really glad you asked that because it's a critical concern that we should talk about.

In summary, vary your cushions, make them conversational, and use them to transition into your answer in a natural way.

Prompters into customer-oriented phrasing are critically important to sales messaging. When we use them, we immediately become more effective and interesting communicators. It is amazing to watch how quickly, in practice coaching sessions, salespeople improve their sales messaging with this simple technique. Examples of customer-oriented prompter phrases would be:

- What our customers like about our approach is …
- What we hear from customers all the time with respect to your question is …
- I was speaking to a customer the other day who told me something that relates directly to your question. What she said was …
- If you were to call some of our customers and ask them that same question, here's what they would tell you …

When we use these phrases RIGHT AFTER THE CUSHION, it immediately gets us into a more interesting communication mode. We're not just sharing our opinion or the opinion of our company; we are talking about what customers think, and that makes a big difference.

In the explain the details step, we get to the heart of our answer. This is where we need to work at understanding our value proposition, competitive advantages, and differentiating factors. We need to weave these factors into a customer-friendly message using customer-oriented phrasing continuously. We'll spend more time on this later in this chapter.

The "T" in CPET = Transition to open ended question, and it's not an exaggeration to say that the entire CPET process is a setup for a great question. *Compete Selling* is about asking better, more provocative questions that PCCRs will engage with. In order to do this, we need a good command of the questions we want to ask. Far too many salespeople make up their questions as the sales interaction develops. This leads to awkward questions or, even worse, to too much talking by the salesperson. After we have explained the details, we need a relevant, open-ended question that ties directly into the message we've just communicated.

The CPET technique is a remarkably simple hack you can use to unlock the magic of your value proposition. It's a better way to weave your competitive advantages and differentiating factors into any answer you give in the sales interaction. Most importantly, it always ends with a good open-ended question, which is critical to controlling the sales process.

While projects with different companies, we've learned that many companies simply don't know their sales messaging, so they can't really teach it to their sales teams. You're not going to be good at the CPET technique, consultative selling or *Compete Selling* until you get your sales messaging down. So, let's look at how you can master it.

Start with headlines. Figure out five to ten short, punchy, and memorable headlines that capture your competitive advantages, the factors that make your company's products and services DIFFERENT from your competitors. For instance, a financial advisor might use:

- Outcomes-based financial planning
- Extreme expertise with trusts and tax reduction strategies
- Relentless focus on protecting capital with safer strategies
- Investments with proven track records
- Continuous review and fine tuning to achieve goals
- Proper balance of growth, wealth protection, and income
- Using money managers with real skin in the game
- (disruptive) We don't follow the herd off the cliff with your money
- (disruptive) Our clients don't believe in the roller coaster approach to investing

The competitive advantages for the digital ad agency example could be:

- Extreme focus on the retail vertical
- Digital analytics that go way beyond market analysis
- Strategies to engage customers into a fantastic buying experience
- Combining digital and traditional approaches to engage a target audience
- More focused advertising where target customers are likely to be
- Ahead of the curve at integrating mobile into your strategy
- (disruptive) Focus on conversion and profitability, not just clicks
- (disruptive) We help our customers sell the way customers want to buy

If you are going to master your sales messaging, you MUST figure out five to ten headlines that convey what makes you, your company, and your products, services, and solutions unique and better than your competitors'. Think of these headlines as the ingredients you're going to "cook" with when communicating that value of your products and services. Some ideas on how to do this would be:

- Organize a conference call with other good communicators in your company and challenge everyone to write down and share a competitive advantage in ten words or less.
- Ask your senior executive(s) to share his or her view of the short headlines about your company's competitive advantages, and what makes your company different from your competitors.
- Read your company's brochures carefully to see what marketing messages might be helpful.
- Talk to the top-performing salespeople in your company and ask them what you asked the senior executive.
- Go to this link on the *Compete Selling* website and go through the sales messaging building exercise. It will help you make progress fast.
- Our consultants and coaches in the SalesGym can help you figure these out if you need help. We do this every day with our clients.

Gather the input and chisel these options down into five to ten short headlines and you'll be in first gear and starting to roll. We kid you not, these headlines are solid gold. You'll use them in a variety of ways throughout the *Compete Selling* sales process. They will give you a significant communication boost in terms of making your message more memorable and persuasive. Without these headlines, you're winging it. *Compete Selling* isn't about making it up as we go along.

The next step is to start working on your CPET responses to some key questions you're likely to get. You need to identify three questions to start out with. The questions we presented earlier in the chapter were:

- Who are you? What do you do? Why does it matter?
- What makes your products and services better or different than your competitors?
- Why should I meet with you when I'm happy with my current supplier/provider?
- What can you give me that I'm not already getting?
- What is your company's value proposition in ninety seconds or less?
- What big, game changing, and disruptive ideas can you introduce to the conversation?

You can probably adapt these to at least get started. It's often a good idea to select your transition question (the fourth step in CPET) FIRST and then make sure everything you say in the first three steps leads naturally into that question. Often, when people try this technique, they just kinda throw an improvised question in there just to end it and it comes off feeling awkward or disjointed and would be hard for a PCCR to respond to. The question is extremely important and needs to tie directly into your message.

Next, we suggest that you use our simple worksheet on competeselling.com to organize your message. Some key reminders to help you craft a better message:

- Think carefully about the question you'll use at the end. Craft the rest of your CPET response to lead naturally into that question.
- Make the cushion as conversational and non-formulaic as possible.
- Use a good customer-oriented prompter phrase right after the cushion.
- Select two or three headlines around which to build your "explain the details" step.
- Use the headlines to introduce the idea, then fill in with more details.
- Be sure to weave customer-oriented phrasing throughout the "explain the details" step.
- Try to focus the "explain the details" step to set up a relevant transition question. The question needs to make sense and to flow naturally from your response.
- Ideally, communicate all of this in less than sixty seconds and never over ninety seconds
- Practice your answers with a good practice partner. Ask your boss, significant other, a friend, or another person on your sales team for help.
- Competeselling.com has more examples that might be helpful for you.
- The practice coaches in the SalesGym are experts at practicing this vital skill.

The Ultra Powerful Three-by-Three Communication Technique

In addition to the CPET technique, another skill you need to master is the three-by-three approach, which you've probably heard countless times. When I learned it, I was told it was first documented by the Greeks over 2,500 years ago as a powerful way to present an argument. There seems to be something about presenting information with three points that just works. Without going into some serious metaphysical woo-woo analysis, it's just an approach that feels right to most people. And, when you tell a person you've got three reasons or three points to make, they'll typically relax and patiently listen to your three points. If you tell them you have ten points to make, you can bet you'll raise their agitation and impatience index. It's even worse when you start an explanation without telegraphing up front how long it will take. That can cause PCCRs to get impatient and tune out or interrupt.

The three-by-three technique is a way to communicate three key points three times, as in:

Now, here's where the work you've done to create your competitive advantages headlines will pay off. Your headlines give you the structure for your three points. Let's see how taking three headlines from the financial advisor example can be used to build a powerful three-by-three value proposition. The three headlines we'll use are:

- Outcomes-based financial planning
- Relentless attention to protecting capital
- Using money managers with real skin in the game

Let's assume we want to communicate our value proposition, and we make a transition with something like:

"What a lot of my clients tell me that makes our approach at Incline Investing so unique really boils down to three key things. First, we use an approach we call outcomes-based financial planning. Second, we are relentless at protecting your capital, and third, we only use money managers with proven track records and real skin in the game.

"What I mean by outcomes-based financial planning is that our clients really like how we start with a complete analysis of their financial goals. We find out what financial independence means to them: how much money they need for retirement, how they hope to fund their children's education, and other objectives they would like to achieve that are going to require capital. Our clients tell us it's much easier to stick to the plan because it's designed to help them get to where they want to go, and to have the money there when they need it for their most important goals. It's your plan, not ours; our role is to help you get there.

"Secondly, I also mentioned our relentless attention to protecting capital. We only recommend investments—regardless of whether these involve stocks, bonds, mutual funds, or other products—that have a very low volatility rating, which means that they perform better when markets are going down. This is critical for your peace of mind, because we've found, over the long haul, these investments perform much better than the high-profile investments that get all the headlines when they're outperforming the market but that get crushed when the markets correct, as they always do.

"Finally, we only select money managers that have a proven track record with real skin in the game. Morningstar's director of research, Russell Kinnell, identifies each year the absolute best of the best in terms of funds. He reveals one of the most powerful indicators of future performance, which is when fund managers have over $1 million of their own money in the fund they manage. This keeps the managers' focus on results. They tend to make better decisions and, remarkably, perform better over time. Our clients really like knowing that the fund managers have their own money invested in their fund.

"To sum up, we first use an approach we call outcomes-based financial planning. Second, we pay extreme attention to protecting capital. And third, we only use money managers with real skin in the game. So, I'm curious about your financial situation. Could you share with me, given how high market prices are right now, what you've done recently to protect your capital in the event of a sharp market downturn?"

Let's analyze what we did here and break it down:

- We started with a quick overview using our three headlines.
- We gave a deeper explanation of each of the headlines one-by-one.
- We used customer-oriented phrasing in each of the deeper explanations.
- After the third point, we summarized with a quick recap of all three headlines.
- We ended with a good open-ended question relevant to one of the headlines.

This three-by-three technique is a fantastic way to make key points that need a little more time and detail to explain. This approach helps make your points in an organized, customer-friendly way that will be much easier to remember.

All of us at the SalesGym believe that practice is the key to becoming a fantastic salesperson who generates top-performer results. To practice, it is helpful to use an organizing worksheet to get started. You can download the three-by-three worksheets at competeselling.com.

Steps to organizing and practicing this technique

- Check out the examples on our website.
- Select three headlines you are going to use.
- Make your introduction of the three ideas with a quick preview.
- Introduce each point you're making in greater detail with customer-oriented phrasing.
- Go through each point one-by-one with more detail using about thirty seconds for each point and utilizing customer-oriented phrasing.
- Summarize at the end with short headlines only (this needs to be quick).
- Have a great question ready at the end that clearly ties into at least one of your headlines.
- Find a practice partner and go through it several times until you can do it without the practice form in a conversational and persuasive way.

The Personal Introduction

A personal introduction is a technique you can use to introduce yourself, when a longer more thorough introduction is called for. It utilizes customer-oriented phrasing and value proposition headlines. This technique is a four-step process:

- Your name and position
- What you specialize in doing
- How your customers benefit
- Transition question

Here's an example of a digital advertising agency salesperson's credibility building personal introduction:

> [name and position] My name is Alan Williams and I'm an account manager for Ultra Matrix Digital Strategies. [what we specialize in doing] We specialize in helping large and small retail companies drive more of the right traffic to their stores and restaurants. Our customers tell us our results are more immediate than typical campaigns they've tried in the past and that our simple measurement tools make decision-making easier. We do this with a deep understanding of how customers use their phones, tablets, and laptops to make quick decisions on where to eat, shop, and seek entertainment. [how our customers benefit] With our strategies, our

customers can get immediate lift in highly profitable impulse traffic and sales, and they can track marketing results and efficiencies in ways that enable them to generate more business with less cost and waste. [transition question] It might be helpful if you could give me a brief introduction of your role at Affluent Restaurant Group as it relates to marketing to generate more traffic ...

Remember, we only use this longer introduction process when we have time for it and it feels like a good fit. Here are a few keys to making it work:

- Tailor it to the person you're meeting with. Make sure you communicate what you specialize at doing in a way that is relevant to the PCCR.
- Use customer-oriented phrasing to bring your introduction to life.
- Have a good question at the end of your credibility statement to transition out of it.
- Try to keep your entire introduction to sixty seconds or less.
- Go to competeselling.com for more examples and worksheets on how to practice your credibility statement.

Every sales professional should be able to deliver an informative, interesting, and memorable quick introduction of themselves when it's needed. The four-step credibility statement is a perfect way to do it.

PRO TIP from Adam Shaivitz

Most of us introduce ourselves many times every day, formally and informally. And we do a fine job. But why be fine? Be extraordinary. Be memorable. A little extra intentional prep goes a long way with intros.

"For example: 'My name is Adam Shaivitz. One of the reasons I'm really looking forward to working with you all is I saw on your website your deep commitment to giving back to your community with your Holiday Helpers program – it really demonstrated a strong team culture. My role will be project manager, so I'll be your main point of contact for regular communication and updates. By way of background, I've lived in LA for seventeen years and originally moved here for business school, where I was a classmate of your colleague Kwame. I also have a twenty-month-old son named Max, so I have lots of project management work at home too.'

"Who am I introducing? Myself, of course. But who do I talk about after mentioning my name ... my audience. That's the counter-intuitive part. Intentionally compliment your audience early in YOUR intro. Be

specific and genuine. It often starts with something like: 'One thing I noticed about your team that was really impressive was …' Or, 'I'm particularly excited to work with this group because …' Most of us feel like we need to build credibility by sharing what we've done. Top performers build credibility by demonstrating how much they know about their audience.

"Other notes from strong intros:

- *When you say your role, explain why they should care about your role and what it means to them. Do you know how many 'account managers' there are out there?*
- *When you share your background, share relevant professional AND personal info (briefly). Does it matter to the project that I have a twenty-month-old son? Not at all. After the meeting, what's the first thing clients usually comment on or ask about? Max. We have something to connect on personally, and we start to build a faster connection, which helps us relate and work together."*

There's more to sales messaging …

There's more to sales messaging covered in upcoming chapters, but if you've gotten your key headlines down, you are well on your way. That's the most important step. When you've got your value proposition key headlines, which are essentially your competitive advantages and differentiating factors, you've got the foundational ingredients you need for the *Compete Selling* process. Don't get too hung up on whether a headline is a differentiating factor or a competitive advantage because it really doesn't matter. The important thing is to have five to ten GREAT headlines that can be crafted into a value proposition, a three-by-three presentation, a credibility building personal introduction or an answer to virtually any question, and, when we get there, insight-led statements that drive the more assertive elements of *Compete Selling.*

You MUST first craft your headlines and then excel at communicating them to master *Compete Selling*. This is one of the most important things that top performers do better than all the rest.

Four

Pre-Call Planning

We've seen a lot of pre-call planning systems, forms, and checklists. Most of them are helpful and well-conceived. However, I sometimes wonder if these systems and forms are put together for the benefit of the training department or the sales managers, because more often than not, sales teams don't use them. Some companies are better than others at getting their sales teams into a pre-call planning model they actually use; but, from our experience in working with a lot of companies, this is the exception and not the rule.

The essential pre-call planning steps we recommend include:

- Make sure you know who will be in the meeting, especially anyone you haven't met before.
- Do some research on new people you're meeting via LinkedIn, the company's website, and other research sources.
- Get your invites and confirmation of the agenda for the meeting out in advance, if possible, and ask for input on it.
- Refresh your memory on any personal details of people in the meeting you've met before, such as where they're from, family situation, where they went to college, hobbies, favorite sports teams, etc.
- Identify the specific outcomes you hope to see in this meeting. It's best to have a stretch outcome and a fallback if the stretch outcome becomes unrealistic.
- If you need to summarize a previous meeting, put your notes together for that.
- Identify three to five (minimum) questions you want to ask, especially provocative ones.
- Determine the two to three questions you would like to be asked. We'll go into why this is so important in a future chapter.
- Determine which techniques you'll use to introduce the more provocative questions so it's done in a positive way. We'll cover this in a future chapter
- Determine what objective, third-party evidence you can use to reinforce the new thinking you are presenting.
- Think through how to make your proposals, ideas, fact sheets, etc., more interesting using customer-focused language.
- Carefully think through how you can use technology in the meeting, and make sure it's absolutely bulletproof.
- Prepare success stories that highlight a decision-maker who made the decisions you are hoping to achieve as your outcomes.

- Practice and rehearse aloud. Most people neglect this because it's time consuming and uncomfortable. If time is limited, at least practice how you'll start the meeting.
- Prepare your logistics (directions/location; coffee/water; technology; etc.).

You may have other steps, including updating your CRM system and preparing presentation materials, slides, and proposals.

We're not going to spend a lot of time in this book going over topics that have been covered many times in the past. We've listed fifteen key areas above that will help you prepare for sales calls in a more effective way. Top performers don't wing it and you shouldn't either. As we work through the rest of the Compete Sales process, you'll clearly see why we have these fifteen steps and how critical they are to a more assertive approach that will work without ruining the relationship.

We'll sum up this short chapter by saying you will not be very successful at the more assertive elements of *Compete Selling* if you do not become disciplined about pre-call planning and practicing. You can view and download a helpful pre-call planning checklist on competeselling.com.

Five

Opening the Call

At the SalesGym, we think of opening the call as everything that happens from the moment you greet your PCCR, either in person, or via phone or video conference, until the moment you bridge into either the discovery or solution presentation step.

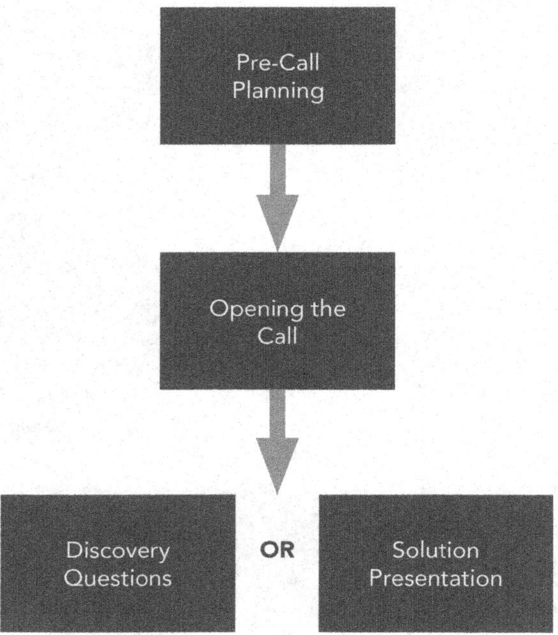

On most sales calls, the first thing on the agenda is to ask questions and learn more about the PCCR's needs. On some calls, though, you've already done some or all of this, so you're coming back to make a solution presentation or demonstration of some sort. Either way, we need to open the call effectively. There are a number of elements that go into that:

- Greeting and preliminary pleasantries
- Bridge from preliminary pleasantries to the agenda
- Introducing and confirming the agenda
- Participant introductions, including your credibility building personal introduction covered in the last chapter, if needed
- Transitioning to the first item on the agenda

Opening the sales interaction the right way will have an enormous impact on results. Top performers approach this early part of the call seriously.

The opening of the call sets the tone and often projects and amplifies your credibility or lack of it. We want to project and amplify the right things, so let's take a look at each of these important steps. Many salespeople are poorly prepared when it comes to opening the call, which is a big mistake.

Greeting and Preliminary Pleasantries

Do you have a good handshake? Are you sure? How do you know? Have ever asked anyone to give you a handshake evaluation? The handshake, smile, and initial greeting are very important. There is no excuse for a poor handshake, but it's amazing how many people can't do it well. We suggest you shake hands with a few people you trust and ask them for honest feedback.

When you look someone in the eyes and tell them, "It's a pleasure to meet you," or, "It's great to see you again," is it sincere? Are you focused and in the moment? Is your smile warm and alive? This seems like pretty basic stuff to think about, but it's extremely important. Projecting confidence with our smile, greeting, handshake, and overall presence as we convey genuine enthusiasm for that moment is a big part of what gives many top-performers their edge. It's not enough to feel excited about meeting our PCCRs, we need to project and communicate enthusiasm in a genuine and appropriate way. A lot of subtle and important impressions and decisions are made in the first ten seconds when we meet someone. Pay attention to it and bring your A game to the first impression.

It can be helpful in your pre-call planning for a first-time meeting with new people to connect a picture with a name. It's essential to get the names of the people you're meeting right and to be able to pronounce them correctly. Don't be afraid to check your pronunciation if it's an unusual name, because that shows you are a competent professional. Pre-call planning can help us get the names right before the meeting starts.

One of the most important elements of preliminary pleasantries is to quickly get into an asking and listening mode. The less you talk about yourself, the better. We've found it's best to have a reliable and consistent approach to the first minute or two. When I meet someone for the first time, I typically ask them:

- Where are you from?
- How long have you been living here?
- What brought you here in the first place?

Usually, with these three questions something will come out that I can connect with and continue asking and listening. I've found it best to keep it light, stay away from any threatening or controversial topics (don't make a comment on politics, for example), and focus on the people we're meeting.

If you've done online research on the person(s) you're meeting, be careful to not mention too much about that research. However, if you want to draw attention to something you noticed, you can do so like this: "While preparing for our meeting today, I ran across an article you wrote on group dynamics that was posted on LinkedIn and I really liked your ideas about how to get tech project teams unstuck when they're bogged down."

When meeting someone a second or third or tenth time, it's still best to get them talking with simple questions like:

- Been doing anything for fun this summer?
- Been traveling much since the last time we met?
- Got any fun trips or vacations planned in the next year?
- How did your son's high school football team do this year?
- Have you been out mountain biking much this year?

It's a great habit to jot down notes about the people you meet, such as the name of their spouse and children, where they went on vacation, how old their kids are, and what their interests are. Then, refer back to these notes in your pre-call planning next time you meet. It really helps to make a great first impression.

Bridge from Preliminary Pleasantries to the Agenda

After a few minutes of preliminary pleasantries, it's important for you to make the transition into the agenda and not wait for your PCCR to do it. The best way to do this is to say something positive about the person or people you're meeting with and then introduce your agenda. Here are a few examples:

- Julie, I was really looking forward to our meeting because I'm always impressed by how focused you and your team are on finding better ways to refine your marketing campaigns. In thinking about our meeting and how to make it most beneficial for you and everyone else in the room, here is the agenda we suggest.
- Bill, last time we got together, you mentioned something that really stuck in my memory. You said that not only does your team need to find a better solution to reduce your security risks, but you need to do it in a

way that doesn't increase costs. As a result of that, the agenda I suggest we use to get the most out of our meeting today would be ...

- Bob and Cheri, I've really been looking forward to meeting you today as you had mentioned on the phone when we set up this meeting that you were interested in ways to cut your tax exposure and to put more money away for your kid's education. I really respect that. What I suggest for our agenda would be ...
- Frank, what really amazed me about you in our last meeting was how focused you are on finding new clients and helping them avoid the legal mistakes that so many partnerships make in the early stages of forming a company. In order for us to get the most out of our time together today, I suggest we use this agenda ...

In summary, say something positive about the person you're meeting with, draw attention to a strength you may have noticed, and show them you put some thought into the agenda. And remember, it's best if YOU make the bridge into the agenda and don't wait for your PCCR to do it. People often ask how long to spend on preliminary pleasantries before transitioning to the agenda. It's a good question without a perfect answer. It can depend on culture or company norms. A decent rule of thumb is to spend about 10 percent or less than the total time allotted for the meeting on pleasantries.

Setting and Confirming the Agenda

After you've transitioned into the agenda, you need to preview your agenda items and get confirmation to move forward. Here's a full range of possible agenda items on a sales call depending on what type of call it is:

- Meet everyone in the room (participant introductions).
- Summarize some key points and follow up from a previous meeting, if applicable.
- Review past performance, results, and insights.
- Ask some questions to get a clearer understanding of their situation/problem/needs.
- Potentially put a real bias or provocative topic into the room.
- Share some ideas that would be helpful to the person(s) you're meeting with.
- Bring a new team member who's at the meeting into the conversation when they have special expertise that can add value.
- Present a solution or proposal based on the last meeting you had.

- Figure out if there's any way to collaborate and discuss possible next steps in that direction.
- And finally, transition to the first item on the agenda.

Depending on the meeting, there may be other agenda items, but this is typically what is covered on most sales calls. At the end of your agenda, you'll want to confirm that the agenda is agreeable before moving forward. Questoins that work well include, "How does that sound?" or, "Does this seem like a good agenda for our meeting and is there anything else we should add to it?"

It's important, right from the start, to use customer-oriented phrasing and avoid saying things like, "What I'd like to do ..." or, "What I'd really like to cover in our meeting ..." That's you focused and not *customer* focused. Instead, use phrases like:

- In thinking about our meeting and to make sure we get the most out of it, I'd suggest we cover the following ...
- In preparing for our meeting, my primary concern is making sure we cover the details that matter most to you. So with that in mind, I'd suggest a good agenda for our meeting today would be ...

This might not seem like a big deal, but it is. Getting into customer-oriented phrasing from the first moment, including taking an active interest in your prospect during preliminary pleasantries, builds trust and rapport, and reduces resistance. It's remarkable, when you sit back and observe, how many salespeople repeatedly say, "What I'd like to do . . ." just in the first few minutes of the call. If you have that habit, break it now.

Meeting Participants Introductions

If you are meeting someone for the first time, or if you are attending a meeting where you only know some of the participants, then make your first agenda item to meet everyone in the room. We've seen this go sideways many times, often because the introductions eat up too much time. This can be a real issue when the meeting involves four or more participants. The best way to avoid this is to communicate a format for introductions. Then start the conversation yourself or have one of your team members take the lead.

For example: "It might be a good idea if we all quickly introduced ourselves, maybe in thirty seconds or so. I'll go first. My name is Michael St. Lawrence and I'm one of the founders of the SalesGym. I've been researching and writing books about and working with top-performing salespeople and sales teams on strategy and training most of my career. That's taken me from Wall Street to Washington, DC to Los Angeles. I've started three consulting companies and I'm really glad to be here meeting with all of you at The Idea Factory, which is one of the coolest company names I've ever heard. Let's just go around the room with some quick introductions. John, could you be next?"

You want to avoid a situation in which the first intro takes way too long. You don't want to hear a complete resume starting with what the person studied in college followed by all the positions he or she had in the past twenty years. That could take two to five minutes. If that happens, then the rest of the people in the room could follow that example while you stress over how much of your meeting time is going down the drain. We suggest you make the first introduction in not more than thirty seconds. That will set the example so everyone gets the message.

On the other hand, when you are meeting a key decision-maker for the first time, or you meet in a formal setting where you make a presentation to a group, it's better to use the detailed credibility building personal introduction we learned in chapter 3 on sales messaging.

You should figure out your agenda, obviously, in pre-call planning; and usually it's a good idea to share it at least a few days before the meeting so everyone has time to prepare.

So, what are the *Compete Selling* elements to "opening the call"?

The focus of this chapter, so far, has been basic consultative selling reminders. *Compete Selling* is unique because it uses better customer-oriented language, and it possibly places a more assertive agenda on the table. An agenda that brings a provocative topic into the meeting would clearly be a *Compete Selling* technique. For instance, consider these agenda items:

- I'd suggest we talk right up front about one of the most critical concerns companies like yours have in terms of doing business with a company like ours, which is: What about our track record and the fact that we've only been in business for three years?
- It might be helpful if we take a look at different ways that companies like yours are determining the best way to select a general contractor to build out your new office.
- Perhaps we should take a look at what other companies like yours are doing in terms of finding and recruiting tech employees. Some are using tactics that are radically different than what's been done in the past.

- I'm eager to share some ideas we've gotten from some innovative firms like yours that are finding better ways to generate risk-adjusted returns that simply aren't based on asset allocation models that have been so trusted over the last thirty years.
- Some companies that are comparing our approach to our competitors are concerned about why we have a reputation for being more expensive. It might be a good idea to cover this today.
- I'd like to review with you some of the suggestions we've received from other clients about mistakes they've made when selecting an accounting firm.
- Most marketing directors we meet wonder how conversion can be increased with a lower budget? This would be a great place for us to start because our approach is quite different from what you're doing now.
- Another topic that might be helpful to you would be to talk about the hidden costs, risks, and consequences of structuring a portfolio around only passive index funds.
- A good fit for our agenda would be to explore some underlying assumptions about how mobile fits into an overall marketing campaign, and the radical changes taking place in how leading companies generate new customers.

Remember, *Compete Selling* is about pushing the boundaries, bringing more assertive topics into the conversation, and moving objections and concerns forward in the sales process. We can do that right in the agenda.

So that's the full story on how to open a call the right way. Too many salespeople don't give enough attention to the first few minutes of the call, and and it's a huge mistake. This is a critically important element of the sales process, and it's relatively easy to make a great first impression with a little effort. It's well worth it. When you start a meeting with a good agenda, it communicates that you're prepared, you're a professional, and you took the time to get ready—all good things to project. Doing these things will enable the people you meet to relax and adjust into your process, which is exactly what you want in *Compete Selling*.

Six

Discovery 2.0

This is going to be a beefy chapter. It takes a lot of skill and practice to ask good questions and to position assertive questions in a way that communicates you want to help without being a high-pressure jerk. Questions will either open up the conversation or annoy the heck out of the person you're meeting with, depending on the way you ask them. We're going to look at at some powerful *Compete Selling* approaches to questioning that will help you become *more assertive in an effective way*, more often, during sales calls.

In general, to be effective at the assertive Compete Selling discovery approaches, you need:

- Absolute command of the headlines (we covered this in chapter 3) around your value proposition, competitive advantages, and differentiating factors
- Questions that lead to your competitive advantages
- A variety of approaches to position questions that are assertive while lowering the confrontation factor
- A clear understanding of the thinking and biases of decision-makers that prevent them from using your product/services
- An interesting way of spicing up your discovery step with insights that cause a shift in thinking or perspective that is beneficial to your competitive advantages
- To be focused on the PCCR, listening and reacting to what is happening in a relevant and engaging way; avoiding formulaic patterns that cause you to be robotic or disengaged from the flow of the conversation

Over the last couple of years, I've interviewed hundreds of sales executives who manage sales forces adding up to more than 150,000 people. When I asked them to tell me the most common sales mistakes they observe, nearly all of them mentioned poor or ordinary questioning skills. They talked at length about the inability of so many salespeople to ask deeper, tougher questions that get to the core issues. This prevents them from seeing bigger selling opportunities. Several mentioned a term they called "discovery fatigue" to illustrate how frustrating it can be for PCCRs when they have to answer the same stiff, formulaic questions over and over from salespeople that use the same approach. They wanted their salespeople to lead more interesting conversations that were engaging and provocative at the same time.

The most common mistake in selling

One thing that has not changed much in the last twenty-five years from observing salespeople on sales calls and going through countless practice simulations with them is that the most common mistake in selling continues to be reacting too quickly to a minor selling opportunity that surfaces during the discovery step. Instead of patiently digging deeper to find out more before responding with solutions and recommendations, salespeople often overreact to the first opportunity that surfaces. In fact, more and more salespeople are getting worse in this area.

The second most common mistake in the discovery step

The second most common mistake in the discovery step is asking questions in a way that feels like an examination, interrogation, or process designed by a data gathering engineer. This occurs when the approach is too formulaic and doesn't follow the flow of the conversation in a relevant and natural way. The most obvious and wrenching example of this is when speaking to a poorly trained person in a call center who is obviously using a script. When a salesperson asks questions in a fixed sequence, it can feel disjointed to the PCCR. Scripted questions often prevent salespeople from using conversational and natural follow-up questions. This questioning style reduces rapport and will often generate guarded or misleading answers. Even worse, it can feel like unwanted pressure to the PCCR.

PRO TIP from Mark Woodland

> *"Most salespeople I talk to think that discovery and asking questions is primarily for them . . . so that they can uncover the 'hot buttons' or 'pain points' they need to 'sell' the PCCR on the value of their solution and why it's perfect for the customer. My experience is that great discovery that asks genuine, sincere questions aimed at understanding the customer and, when appropriate, using provocative questions that challenge the customer's thinking does more to get the customer ready to 'hear' the solution than anything else. You can build more credibility, demonstrate world-class industry knowledge, and get a PCCR ready to say yes, (and secretly thinking: 'Wow this guy really gets it; he really understands what makes us different.') by asking great questions than 'pitching' any day of the week."*

Fishing with a big net instead of a single line

A good way to think about the discovery step is that all too often, salespeople use questions the way a fisherman might fly fish, casting out a lure and looking for a bite. When the bite happens, he reacts quickly to try and hook the fish and reel him in. In other words he's reacting to the first nibble that surfaces in the sales process.

A better way to approach discovery is to think of it as trolling the area with a big net, fishing a large area BEFORE pulling the net up to see what's been caught. This way, we discover more opportunities. Then, when we pull up the net, we decide which fish or opportunity to go after, which is ideally the biggest, meatiest fish in the catch. "Fishing with a net" is like asking a variety of questions without overreacting. Instead of immediately jumping into sales mode, it's better to listen patiently, taking notes and waiting until we gain a complete understanding through our assertive questioning process.

The decision maker does not have to be honest with you

It's critical to keep in mind that the buyer does not have to be honest with you when answering your questions. Many buyers believe they need to use a certain degree of deception to negotiate the best possible deal. The degree of honesty and candor is largely determined by trust and rapport. Once the buyer begins to doubt doing business with you, he will tilt his answers in a way that make it more difficult for you and easier for him to get you out of the way with as little confrontation as possible. As such, our questions always need to be interesting, relevant, conversational, thought provoking, and trust building.

The ultimate "winging it" area of the sales process

Questioning, for whatever reason, also seems to be an area in which many salespeople like to work freestyle. They often depend on natural conversation abilities to come up with good questions on the fly, and this is one of their biggest mistakes. Although this approach can make the interaction more conversational, it all too often leads to missed opportunities because the salespeople don't have a basic plan for going into the discovery step. The more common mistake, however, is they simply talk too much and ask too little. Bottom line is, you need your headlines for sales messaging and you need questions that tie into the headlines. Without them, you're going to miss opportunities, get caught up in the moment, overreact to early opportunities, and talk too much instead of listening.

Our favorite consultative selling questioning flow

Because we train and practice with salespeople every day in the SalesGym, we hear lots of approaches to asking questions. We often hear questions that seem random, stiff, or disconnected from a logical progression in the conversation. When this happens, the PCCR usually gets turned off and feels like he or she is being interrogated or not being listened to. So, the questioning process needs to follow a natural flow that makes sense in terms of a conversation. This means that the sequence of the questions is as important, if not more so, than the questions themselves. For most salespeople the sequence shown below is very effective in engaging with a PCCR.

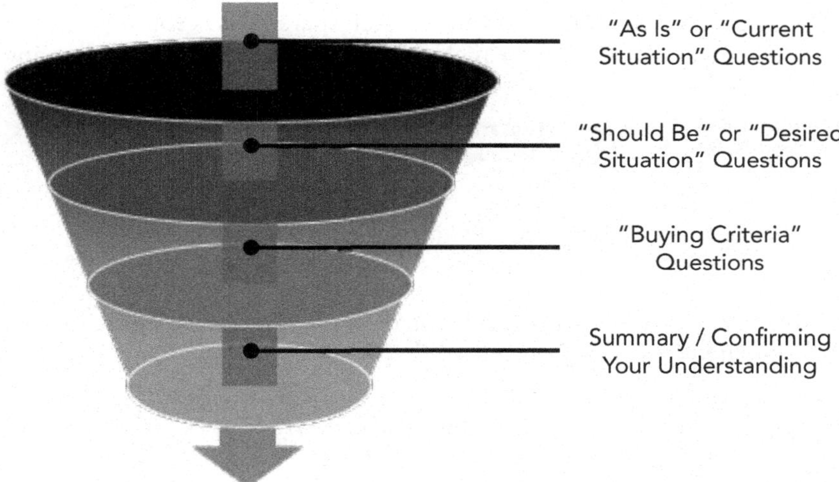

This is a simple, but effective diagnostic flow that helps identify what changes need to happen to get the PCCR to where they want or need to go. Although the steps are simple, there's nothing simple at all about asking engaging questions that help the decision-maker verbalize their current situation and the changes they would like to make that line up well with your competitive advantages..

This questioning flow works best when:

- The PCCR is committed to being as honest with you as they are with your competitors
- The PCCR understands what he needs and why
- The PCCR is looking for advice and is open to different approaches to solving his or her problems
- The buyer has not formed inflexible buying criteria that don't line up with your competitive advantages

- The PCCR does not have any strong biases for your competition's differentiating factors
- The PCCR is aware of how important your competitive advantages are in solving his or her problems

Consultative selling questioning can come up short

Let's take a closer look at how consultative selling questioning, which relies on the PCCR to know what they want, can come up short. For an illustration of this, let's imagine our Ultra Matrix digital ad salesperson asks some questions of Barbara, the owner of the seven high-end restaurants in Los Angeles and see what happens:

Digital Ad Salesperson's Questions	Barbara's Answers
Tell me a little about the campaigns you've used this last six months?	
	They're similar to what have worked well for us over the last ten years. We tried some new commercials that didn't seem to work.
Could you tell me a little more about what you mean by "they didn't seem to work"?	
	We've seen a slow, but steady decline of new customers coming into our restaurants. We need some ads that will get more customers in the door.
How long has this slow steady drop off been happening?	
	For the last two years. Prior to that, we were experiencing steady growth, but things have really flattened out.
Are there any other factors to which you can attribute the drop off?	
	It's gotta be the ads. We need a new approach. We know that TV and radio work because they've worked for us in the past.

What would represent an acceptable increase in business that would prove to you that this new campaign is working?

We'd like to see a 10 percent increase in new customers over the next quarter.

Have you made any changes in the last two years that might shed some light on why business is off from an advertising standpoint?

We've actually tried two new agencies that came in with new campaigns that looked great, but just didn't get the results.

Tell me about those campaigns, if you would?

We actually increased our spend by 10 percent on both radio and TV, but the commercials just didn't drive the traffic we thought they would. Interestingly, we've heard some good things about the commercials from our loyal customers.

So, just to verify, you're really looking for some new commercials and a strategy to drive better results?

That's right. We tried a few small tests like digital ads on Facebook and Google, but I didn't see much in terms of results, so we'd like to stick with radio and TV.

What did you try in terms of digital strategies?

We decided to put about 10 percent of our budget into digital ads that would focus on younger customers, but it didn't pay off. So, I think we need to cut our spend there and focus more on TV and radio.

In this example, our consultative sales professional is asking lots of good, open-ended questions. He's listening and asking relevant follow-up questions. Based on what he's learning, his solution will probably need to be based on TV and radio ads, because that's what the owner, Barbara, thinks she needs. Barbara is likely to make another poor decision focused only on TV and radio and ignore the big advantage that well-targeted digital ads could give her. She simply doesn't know what she doesn't know. Consultative selling is largely about finding out what the customer wants and finding a way to give that to them better than the competitors.

Now, let's take a look at some assertive questions, asked in a somewhat blunt and awkward way, along with some hypothetical responses.

Digital Ad Salesperson's Assertive Questions	Barbara's Answers
Have you considered that maybe TV and radio ads aren't producing the results they used to because of the changes in the way people look for places to eat?	
	We thought about that, but we don't think that's it. Our customers tell us they found us through our TV and radio ads. They really like them.
Maybe you should consider increasing your digital ad allocation to get better results?	
	I think that would be a waste of money because it didn't work well over the last couple of quarters.
Maybe some of the underlying assumptions that have worked for you for years just don't work the way they used to. Have you considered that fewer people are watching TV and listening to traditional radio now than they did even two years ago?	
	With TV, we can capture the atmosphere and visuals of our restaurants and food. That's what really attracts people. I attended a marketing conference last year that showed TV can get even better results if it is done right.
What we're finding is that a more balanced approach to digital along with TV and radio can really complement one another and produce better results. Can you see how that might work better than your current strategy?	
	I think I told you already that we just didn't get the results with the digital experiments we were hoping for. Doesn't make sense to me to increase spending without the underlying proof it will work. I don't feel like you're listening to what I'm telling you and I'm losing my patience.

As you can see, the assertive questions are raising the emotional temperature and increasing Barbara's defensiveness, which is why being assertive without proper approaches doesn't always work, and can easily backfire.

The Compete Selling, assertive questioning approaches

Assertive questions can be invasive and threatening. As a result, they can be more risky. They introduce potential conflict and confrontation into the interaction. It takes more finesse and interpersonal skills to ask them without being offensive. The success of the assertive style has a lot to do with how HASP sellers ask questions. They typically ask more questions about the buyer's decision-making criteria and beliefs. If this is not done skillfully, it can come across as overly invasive and confrontational; it can feel, to the PCCR, that the salesperson is criticizing her thinking. This can cause a defensive reaction and a breakdown of trust and rapport. It's important to note that if assertive approaches get you better information but destroy trust and rapport, you could win the battle but lose the war (the sale).

The real art of *Compete Selling* is being able position and set up our questions so they feel less threatening and are more interesting to respond to while allowing the buyer to reveal his or her biases.

Three techniques to set up a question

Let's look at three different techniques to set up a question. Keep in mind, the goal is to soften a provocative question in a way that is easier to respond to, is less threatening, and is less likely to cause a defensive, trust-lowering response. These approaches can also help you project more credibility, professionalism, and competence, which can have a positive impact on the PCCR's willingness to offer honest responses. The three approaches are:

Conventional vs. Contrasting Thinking focused on Decision-Making Criteria

- We briefly explain conventional thinking, which is often similar to the limited thinking of the buyer. Then we compare that with the innovative and forward thinking we seeing from other customers. Then we ask the PCCR to react to the comparison.

The Observation-Based Question

- We set up our provocative question with an observation that is relevant to one of our competitive advantages.

Tee-Up: "A question I often get . . ."

- Introducing a question we often get and then answer that question with the CPET process.

Let's look at some examples of these approaches in action. The first scenario will involve Barbara, who owns the high-end restaurants. During the first few discovery questions, it became clear early on that she understood TV and radio, was comfortable with those media, and was looking for an agency that could design a better campaign that would stop the sharp decline in her advertising results. The salesperson realized that he had a low chance of making a sale based on a better strategy for TV and radio ads. More importantly, the salesperson knew that better results could be obtained by increasing digital solutions. He realized that she was technology resistant, and he wanted to challenge her belief that a 90 percent emphasis on TV and radio was the best strategy. In this example, he positions assertive questions to get Barbara to consider a new way of thinking about her advertising approach without telling her she's wrong.

Conventional vs. Contrasting Thinking Question Set Up	Barbara's response to this *Compete Selling* Approach

*Barbara, **conventional thinking we've heard for years** from very successful retail entrepreneurs like you is that radio, TV, and print have worked well in the past. They hit a wide range of people and do a great job of keeping your name out there in the marketplace. We're also hearing some contrasting thinking from retail business owners whose businesses are growing rapidly. Despite the obvious challenges, they're rethinking mobile. Although business "location" still matters, it's about being able to contact customers based on THEIR "location." They're using mobile to target nearby consumers. **What's your take on the best way to capitalize on mobile, in terms of contacting customers who are close to your restaurants?***

We tried digital marketing in the past that really didn't produce very good results, but we didn't really focus on mobile. I thought radio was the best way to reach people on the go, but I guess people do rely on their phones now. Sometimes people make reservations twenty or thirty minutes before they show up to eat. They also seem to pay attention to our online reviews.

The Observation-Based Question Approach	Barbara's response to this *Compete Selling* Approach

*Barbara, just last week, I was talking to an owner of several furniture stores who told me that for years he has used traditional media because his customers knew him and just needed TV and radio reminders. He hasn't stopped TV and radio entirely, but he has shifted a large portion of his budget to mobile and social media because he realized how many people he can get to visit when they're "in the neighborhood." More people are making quick decisions today, spontaneously entering his stores, and buying. **What's your take on the best way to capitalize on mobile, in terms of contacting customers who are close to your restaurants?***

That kind of targeting would probably work for us, especially with tourists looking for special offers and interesting new cocktails. Tell me more about how you can get to these customers better than the results we got in the past?

The Tee-Up: "A question I often get ..."	Barbara's response to this *Compete Selling* Approach

Barbara, a question I often get from long-time, successful business owners like you who have focused on TV and radio is, "How do I become familiar with all the data and complexity of digital advertising?" (Watch how we use the CPET technique.) It's a good question, because it is different. In fact, the best retailers tell us it's different in a good way. First of all, you can dial-up your presence and advertise more to people close to your restaurants during slower days and times; and you can change your messaging to make it more relevant, such as offering lunch specials during the day and drink specials later in the afternoon. This is all targeted at people who are nearby and most likely visit. Our team manages all the data for you so your decision-making is easy. ***So, what's your take on the best way to capitalize on mobile, in terms of contacting customers who are close to your restaurants?***

Hmmm, it would be nice to capture these spontaneous customers on our less busy evenings. Right now, we're not getting the kind of impulse decision traffic we need or even what we used to get. What you're saying is interesting.

Same question in all three examples

You probably noticed we used the same assertive question that challenged Barbara's base assumption, but set it up in three different ways. This is one of the most important things to understand about assertive *Compete Selling* questioning approaches. We need to ask the tough questions in a way that is less offensive and easier to respond to without causing the buyer to feel threatened, insulted, or wrong. It's all based on presenting insights and ideas that are working better than their ideas or biases. After explaining why, we then ask them to react to the contrast. In Barbara's case, we know three key things about her:

- She wants more customers and is disappointed with her advertising strategy results.
- She is not comfortable with digital advertising because she doesn't understand it.
- She got great results with radio and TV ads in the past, but for the last two years the results have been declining.

We want her to consider new ideas without telling her she's wrong, stupid, or misinformed. That's what these approaches do for us. They give Barbara a way to react to the ideas of other business owners and not feel she has to defend her ideas or admit she's wrong.

Let's take a look at another salesperson who sells innovative, boutique mutual funds, including an atypical real estate growth fund. This fund is unusual because, unlike most real estate funds that are used for monthly income, this fund provides growth similar to stock funds. He is calling on a financial advisor who manages the accounts of many wealthy individuals. He wants the PCCR to consider a new fund for some of his clients as a safer way to get growth than stocks. But this advisor only uses bond funds to generate monthly income for his clients.

The conventional vs. contrasting thinking approach

"John, the conventional thinking we've heard for years from successful advisors like you is that it's best to blend real estate in client portfolios with bonds to generate income. Real estate is a great way to increase monthly income, particularly for retirees, and it also pays well to the advisor. However, we're hearing some contrasting thinking from advisors who are finding new and innovative ways to use commercial real estate, which is less volatile than the stock market, to generate growth. This approach is working well to get money off the sidelines. It is a less volatile strategy that has generated low teens risk adjusted returns over the last twenty years, returns that were typically only reserved for institutional investors but that are now available to retail investors. I'm curious, John, how could a less volatile approach to growth help you approach some of your investors who are nervous about the stock market and have too much money on the sidelines in cash?"

The observation based question approach

"John, last week I was talking to an advisor who was concerned about a number of his clients who had too much cash on the sidelines and had missed out on this fantastic bull market. He started trying a new approach to growth using commercial real estate in a way that large institutional clients have used for years. It's less volatile than the stock market and is an easier choice for investors who are more comfortable with real estate than stocks. I'm curious, John, how could a less volatile approach to growth help you with your investors who are nervous about the stock market and have too much cash on the sidelines?"

The "a question I often get" question tee up

"John, a question I've been getting from a number of advisors recently is, what are other advisors doing to get more money off the sidelines and into the market when investors are scared to death of the stock market, especially at today's lofty levels and geopolitical uncertainty? (Here comes the CPET!) It's a great question because there is still a ton of nervous money on the sidelines. We're seeing some successful advisors who have big books of business use commercial real estate in a new way. They're using a new fund that invests in real estate for growth instead of income. They like telling this story to investors because the fund manager has a twenty-year track record of returning mid-teens performance to large institutional investors. Now he's started a fund that retail investors can use. They're finding that investors with too much money in cash like this commercial real estate approach. I'm curious, John, how could a less volatile approach to growth help you assist some of your investors who are nervous about the stock market and have too much cash on the sidelines?"

Once again, same question in all three examples

Our mutual fund salesperson is introducing a somewhat controversial idea, which is new to most advisors. He is trying to create a change in thinking that taps into a few of the advisor's problems:

- He has investors who are afraid of the stock market, hold way too much in cash, and are missing out on potential returns.
- He needs new ideas to get his investors' money off the sidelines and into investments that will grow faster than cash and low interest paying bond funds.

This approach introduces a change of thinking by using customer-oriented phrasing that taps into what other successful advisors and investors are doing.

Let's look at these three approaches more closely

Conventional vs. contrasting thinking

- The first step is to identify a few questions you'd like to ask that are assertive and tied into your value proposition and competitive advantages.
- We start with conventional thinking by sharing what other people, similar to the PCCR, are doing and have done for years. This ideally reflects the thinking of the PCCR.
- We communicate this conventional thinking in a neutral way, not negatively or critically.
- After we present the conventional thinking, we introduce contrasting thinking, again with customer-oriented phrasing from other buyers who

are approaching this topic in a different, more effective way. We present what they are doing in a somewhat neutral way, but we emphasize the results they're getting. This is typically based on the thinking of our best customers who are already aligned with our value proposition.

- We finish with a question that allows the PCCR to react to these two contrasting approaches. Typically the choice is between older and tired vs. new, innovative, and producing better results.

The observation-based question approach

- Think of this as a shorter, slimmed down version of conventional vs. contrasting thinking. We are essentially presenting the contrasting thinking so it comes out quicker.
- We use customer-oriented phrasing to communicate an observation about what other buyers are doing that is different from what the PCCR is doing. We present the results they're getting and then conclude with a question that asks the PCCR to respond.

Tee-Up: "A question I often get . . ."

- This is a fantastic way to add some energy to the discovery step when you feel it is stalled and you need to say something to spice it up.
- This approach is very effective at bringing a likely objection or concern forward in the conversation. HASPs do this because the worst time to address concerns or objections is at the end of the sales process.
- In most cases, PCCRs do not ask the questions we hope to be asked. This technique is perfect for bringing great questions into the conversation.
- We get it started, typically when the conversation needs a little energy, by introducing a question that taps DIRECTLY into one of our competitive advantages.
- We use the CPET technique to answer the question and end it with a good open-ended question to dive back into discovery.

All three approaches

Using all three approaches allows us to react and respond in the discovery step without selling or jumping on an opportunity too fast. Often, the discovery step can feel stalled if the PCCR is not responding with open answers. If we keep drilling with question after question, it can feel awkward. These techniques allow us to introduce new insights and ideas, in a comfortable and conversational way, for the PCCR to react to. These ideas represent a different point of view than the PCCR's perspective, which is exactly what we want. We challenge their current opinions and thinking by bringing new thinking into the conversation, not by criticizing or making the PCCR feel wrong. This approach will help the PCCR discover new ideas and approaches in a less defensive way.

These approaches feel more conversational

An important advantage of using these question positioning techniques is that they help the conversation feel more relaxed. They enable natural give and take instead of a flurry of one-way questions that feel stiff and forced. These techniques give us a way to say interesting things in the discovery step without disrupting the flow or going into a product presentation too early in the process. Often, we meet with PCCRs who are not very talkative and who give us short answers that are hard to work with. These question setup approaches can prime the pump to get a conversation rolling.

These approaches bring OUTSIDE THINKING into the conversation

This is important. Salespeople often talk a lot during sales calls about how they think, how their company thinks, and why their company is right or better. This can cause a defensive reaction because the PCCR is doubtful that salespeople are honest brokers of information. After all, they're paid by their companies to say the things they do. With these three approaches, we're bringing in the thinking of other customers. That is usually less threatening and more interesting to a PCCR. If it's done right, the PCCR will identify with how other customers think and be more open in answering assertive questions.

PRO TIP from Adam Shaivitz

> *We need to first earn the right to be selfish with our questions. Here's a possible question I might ask with the types of PCCRs I meet with:*
>
> *"What are your sales training priorities for this next year?"*

As you know, I sell sales training and practice via the SalesGym. So you might imagine I ask questions like the one above to sales leaders. You're correct, I do. But how does that question impact the way I'm perceived? Most of us have been taught that if we're asking questions, then we're being client-centric and consultative. But are we? Why am I asking the question above? Is it for my interest or for my client's?

Let's say my client, Melissa, oversees a large sales organization at a digital media company. Melissa, like most sales leaders, is responsible for performance, growth, recruiting, collaborating with marketing and product development … and, oh yes, training. So when I start a conversation with her and early on I ask: "What are your sales training priorities for this next year?" Is that an "Adam question" or a "Melissa question"? Remember, Adam's entire professional world is focused on "sales training" and Melissa runs a team and business, so training maybe accounts for 5 to 10 percent maximum of what she cares about professionally. So starting off with that narrow and specific question, demonstrates I'm looking out for myself and I have something to sell. Asking about Melissa's sales training priorities is a selfish question. Now, if I want to be an effective salesperson, I need to be thoughtful and selfish at times, but I need to earn the right to get there. Look at this version of questioning with Melissa:

- I know when we last spoke, you mentioned huge priorities to grow your mobile and video businesses. How's that going?
- Where are your bright spots here? Where are you seeing success?
- With which clients?
- Which teams and sellers are having the most success growing their mobile and video efforts.
- What are they doing better or differently?
- What types of conversations would you like to see more sellers and teams practicing to support the continued growth of the mobile and video businesses?

In this flow, my last question (my sixth one) was about the conversations Melissa wants to see sellers practicing. Is that a selfish question? Absolutely. I'd argue it's very similar to the original selfish question about her sales training priorities. But here it works. I've earned the right to ask a selfish question because I've started with more customer-oriented questions about what's most important to Melissa, my client. This question is an appropriate question, but not an appropriate first question.

In an upcoming meeting, when you prepare and plan your questions, consider the sequence. "Selfish" questions can work, but they're usually much more impactful in improving your credibility and the way you're perceived if you've earned the right to ask them, by starting with broader, customer-oriented questions.

Planning worksheets online

We have put together some good worksheets on competeselling.com that can help you with all three of these approaches. They are powerful, and the more you prepare and practice using them, the more doors they'll open for you. Remember, it's not just about asking assertive and provocative questions; it's about asking them in a way that builds trust and introduces new and better insights that can help your PCCR see a new way of thinking that lines up with your value proposition in a natural and conversational way.

Develop questions and positioning approaches around objections!

One big difference between *Compete Selling* and consultative selling is that with consultative selling, objections typically come up late in the process AFTER the PCCR has been presented a solution. With *Compete Selling*, we move the objections up in the process, ideally into the discovery step. We must develop questions and positioning approaches that bring the customer's likely objections and biases into the conversation. The "A question I often get tee-up approach" is perfect for this. Make the question you often get an objection. For instance:

- Bill, one question I often get is why investors who are nervous about the market would even consider adding more real estate to their portfolios?
- Barbara, one question I got recently that relates to our conversation today is: Why is mobile advertising creating better results now than it did even one year ago?
- John, one question we get all the time is: Why are companies making dramatic budget increases to food services for employees when so many other companies are finding ways to cut those costs?

PRO TIP from Ross Robinson

"Great selling is all about talking to clients about what interests them; however, when we ask assertive questions about things like budgets or timelines, we can seem less client-focused and more you/sales-focused. To prevent that, top salespeople often use the phrase, 'So that...' followed by a benefit. 'So that I can put together a proposal that fits within your financial needs, what is the range of your budget for this project?' Or, 'So that I can make sure we allocate the appropriate resources for you, when do you want the solution in place?' Let them know how they will benefit from answering your assertive question.

Questions need to connect to our sales messaging headlines

To begin the process of getting better at questioning, we need to organize some questions around our sales messaging headlines that lead to those strengths. For instance, one of the competitive advantages of the digital ad agency might be:

Strategies to engage customers into a fantastic buying experience

Questions that tie directly into this competitive advantage might be:

- If you could, please tell me how your marketing strategy is tied into the buying experience?
- How do you think your customers would describe their buying experience with your company, from the moment they see the first ad?
- How integrated is your team's sales approach with the marketing messaging that is driven through your social media campaigns?
- Could you show me the process you use to map out the ideal buying experience in relation to the design of your marketing campaigns?

Let's look at some questions designed around a competitive advantage that a mutual fund investment company might have:

Less risky approach to fixed income bond funds

- What kind of high-yield bonds and derivatives are in the fixed income funds you are recommending to your retired clients?
- When was the last time you did a check-up to determine how correlated your fixed income recommendations are to the stock market?
- If the stock market was to enter an extended bear market and drop up to 25 percent, how would that impact the value of your retired investors' fixed income capital?
- In the event of a severe market correction, what would you consider most important in selecting your income-producing bond funds: the total yield or the preservation of capital? Why?

Consultative selling questions tend to focus on things like:

- What are your needs?
- What do you value most in choosing this product/service?
- What problems are you trying to solve with this new product/service?

Assertive, *Compete Selling* questions tend to focus on:

- What do you think about newer, more innovative ways to solve this problem than you've typically chosen in the past?
- How is your current thinking preventing you from finding better solutions?
- How aware are you of different buying criteria or values that might lead you to a better decision?
- How is your current thinking exposing you to risks you may not be aware of?
- How open are you to a more effective way of solving this problem?

To some extent, provocative questions edge into the space of confronting the buyer with the possibility his or her thinking, buying criteria, and basic assumptions are wrong. That's risky. Remember, the buyer doesn't have to buy from you.

So, to summarize the *Complete Selling,* assertive approach to asking questions ...

- The best approach to getting better results in the discovery step is to blend consultative and HASP approaches. We need them both.
- You need a strategy for the flow of your questions that is natural, conversational, and effective.
- You must have your competitive advantage headlines NAILED in order to be effective at this step.
- You need to build a master list of questions that tie directly into your value proposition, competitive advantages, and differentiating factors.
- You need to ask questions that tie into the buyer's likely objections or into the perceived weaknesses they might see in your company, products, or services.
- You need to prepare and PRACTICE using the three techniques to position and tee-up the assertive and provocative questions.

Step-by-step: How to get better at assertive discovery questions

- Get your five most important competitive advantages chiseled into headlines that are ten words or less, with more detail added in a short paragraph.
- Come up with three to five open-ended questions that lead toward each

of these competitive advantages.

- Figure out how you would use the three questioning positioning approaches: conventional vs. contrasting thinking; an observation or insight plus a question; "A question I often get is . . ." sentence to set up all of those questions.
- Finally, using the consultative call flow, arrange these questions in a logical manner that starts with understanding the PCCR's current situation and then develop the desired situation and buying criteria questions.
- Honestly identify the most frequent objections and concerns PCCRs have about your company, products, and services, and figure out a way to bring those concerns into the conversation early in the discovery process. The "A question I often get . . ." approach is perfect for this.

Seven

The Discovery Summary

We've given the discovery summary its own chapter because it's that important. It's remarkable how often we meet salespeople during training events or in coaching sessions at the SalesGym who have been to several training programs on consultative selling but who rarely use a discovery summary as part of their sales process.

Recently, I worked with over five hundred salespeople from one of the country's largest financial institutions. Most of the sales team had at least five years of tenure and more than ten years total of sales experience. All of them had been through at least three different programs on selling, but less than 10 percent of them knew what a discovery summary was. This reminds us how important it is to review the most important steps of consultative and HASP-style selling.

Here are some key things to remember about the discovery summary

- After we have asked a variety of questions and feel we have a good understanding of the PCCR's situation, we briefly repeat a summary of what we heard and ask if we have missed anything.
- The discovery summary is used to pivot into either a solution presentation or a recommendation for a next step.
- The discovery summary shows the PCCR we're listening.
- Very few people can do an effective discovery summary without taking good notes.
- The discovery summary projects competence and professionalism.
- The discovery summary lowers resistance and increases receptivity.
- You will consistently get better results on sales calls if you learn, practice, master, and use summaries on every sales call.

When the discovery summary is done right, it:

- Focuses on things the PCCR said that are helpful to the outcomes we're trying to create
- Is concise and to the point
- Is communicated in a neutral, somewhat positive way
- Gives the PCCR a good opportunity to add more information to further clarify the situation

The discovery summary has three distinct parts

1. Transition into the summary
2. A concise summary that highlights key things the PCCR has said, ideally that connect to your competitive advantages
3. A summary ending that confirms your understanding, and asks for more details to further clarify the situation

A discovery summary example with Barbara the restaurant owner

(Step One) "Barbara, to confirm that I understand your situation, I'd like to quickly summarize what I've learned. Please feel free to correct anything I may have gotten wrong or am missing. (Step Two) You've built a strong customer base over the last twenty-five years by using radio and TV to get your message out and to reinforce your high quality and trendy image to affluent customers. You like how your high visibility advertising has made your restaurants well-known here in Los Angeles. You also love seeing and hearing your advertisements on TV and radio because it gives you constant confirmation that your message is getting out there. In addition, you've seen a steady drop-off of new customers over the last three quarters and a pretty steep one in the last quarter. You haven't spent much on digital because you don't trust it and don't understand how to measure it. Although you personally don't use social media, you realize that people are on their mobile phones constantly, including your kids!, and that we can use mobile to target based on location. You also have certain days and evenings that are much more crowded than others, and you believe this presents a key opportunity. Finally, you want a new strategy that is going to drive growth so you can ultimately open three new restaurants over the next two years. (Step Three) Barbara, what else would you add to this summary to clarify your situation even more for me?"

A discovery summary example with the mutual fund salesperson

(Step One) "John, to confirm that I understand your situation, I'd like to quickly summarize what I've learned. Please feel free to correct anything I may have gotten wrong or am missing. (Step Two) Currently you're using a few different real estate REITS for income with some of your more sophisticated investors. You've never really considered real estate as an investment for growth and are curious how it works. You have at least a third of your investors that are overly conservative in terms of their fears about the market, mostly because of volatility. They feel they've already missed out and don't want to get in now when the market is at such high prices. You think some of your investors understand real estate better than stocks and equities and might feel more comfortable if they felt the real estate investments had a strong track record. You're somewhat concerned that the fees and expenses in a real estate fund might be too high and raise eyebrows with your investors. (Step Three) John, what else would you add to this summary to clarify your situation even more for me?"

We emphasized points that tie into competitive advantages

It's essential, when summarizing, that you begin the process of linking the PCCR's interests and concerns to YOUR competitive advantages.

The best way to end the summary

A lot of sales professionals that do use discovery summaries end them with a question like this:

- Is there anything I missed?
- Did I get that right?
- How does that sound? Does that describe your situation accurately?

These types of questions are certainly better than not using a summary at all, but there's a better way to end the discovery summary. Instead of asking for confirmation that you got it right, ask for more clarification and make it easy for the PCCR to give you more details. For instance:

- John, what else would you add to this summary to clarify your situation even more for me?
- Barbara, so that I can understand your situation even more clearly, what else would you add to this summary?
- If you could, Bill, what have I missed that you could help clarify even further to more accurately reflect your thinking?

If you end your discovery summary this way, you'll find that your PCCR will be much more likely to add information, and you can bet the ranch that whatever they add will be important.

Take notes

Most of us need to take notes if we have any hope of giving a good summary, especially when the discovery questions last more than ten minutes. Sometimes, discovery can take hours to complete. There are a number of different opinions on taking notes and in some companies, it's fine to whip out a laptop or tablet and start typing away. To some PCCRs, this can feel awkward. Usually, taking notes on a simple pad of paper is the best way.

There are different approaches to taking notes, such as mind-mapping, that might be helpful for you to explore if your note taking ability needs improvement.

We cannot emphasize this enough

If you want better results on sales calls, you must ask great questions. This can be accomplished by setting up with the positioning technique you learned in chapter 6, taking good notes, and using discovery summaries. The discovery summary is the best way to pivot from asking and listening into the solution presenting phase of the process. The discovery summary lowers resistance and gets you into the habit of asking, listening, and clarifying which is the best way to get a full understanding of the PCCR's situation.

A discovery is also the perfect way to pivot into your solution (or presentation) of how you can help the PCCR. That's our next chapter.

It is important to practice

You must practice going through the discovery process, taking good notes that tie into your competitive advantages, and giving a great and relevant discovery summary. Many of our clients find the SalesGym the perfect place to work on these skills.

PRO TIP from Emily Knott

I went into banking at the age of twenty-one not having a clue that it was a sales job. Boy, was I surprised when all of a sudden I had sales goals! For some unknown reason, I thrived. I could sell, up-sell, cross-sell, you name it - I made it happen! It wasn't until over a decade later and many other sales jobs and years of consulting that I found myself attributing my success to a single distinguishing factor that I often see in other successful salespeople: genuine curiosity. You will find you have more rewarding sales interactions if you can find a way to be genuinely curious about the person or company you are interacting with. This single mindset gives you the desire to actually listen, the natural ability to be conversational and truly consultative, and when combined with planning and using appropriately assertive questions can alone lead to huge success!"

Emily really nailed it. When we ask questions with natural curiosity, it creates the right atmosphere for a more open and trusting dialogue. Competeselling.com has some worksheets that can improve your questioning process. Remember, the most common mistake in selling is talking too much and not asking good questions. Develop the most important skill that HASPs have: the ability to use provocative, assertive questions in an effective way. That's the best way to generate the kind of answers that lead to a great discovery summary. A great discovery summary paves the way for a better presentation of your solution, one that has a much better chance of succeeding.

Eight

Paradigm Busting Solutions

In this chapter, we'll present some ideas that might be new to you, but we'll keep it moving fast. The solution presentation is a big area that could easily generate a five-hundred page book on its own. Our goal with this book, however, is to keep it short and simple so you won't get bogged down and not finish it. We have worksheets and checklists for you online to help you plan and deliver better ideas, solutions, presentations, and proposals. Let's start by quickly previewing all of the key information in this chapter.

- The entire solution presentation should be based on the discovery summary. The summary lays out the opportunity. If you don't uncover some opportunity in your summary, your chances of making a sale are significantly reduced.
- Benefits are more important than features, and they're even more powerful when they're presented with customer-oriented phrasing that is linked to the needs you highlighted in your discovery summary.
- Ideally, you should identify the PCCR's objections and concerns in the discovery step, so that you can address them in your solution presentation.
- A wide variety of evidence, both from your company and third-party objective sources, is a key element of *Compete Selling*. Your presentation must address the question: Who says so besides you? (WSSBY).
- Examples of how other customers are using your products/services, including information about their ROI, are a key part of a dynamic *Compete Selling* solution.
- Objection and competitor vaccinations are an important tool for making the PCCR more aware of your competitors' shortcomings.
- It's essential, if you want to be more assertive, to make the PCCR more aware of the risks, costs, and consequences of his or her current thinking and decisions; but we need to do it in a kind way that doesn't accuse the PCCR of being wrong.
- Technology is great for AMPLIFYING your message. Find the technology that's a good fit for your audience, rehearse using it, and make sure it works flawlessly during your presentation. Technology hiccups and snafus destroy many sales opportunities.
- The best salespeople learn how to tap into helpful company resources. That often means bringing others into follow-up meetings to move the sale forward. When this is the case, pre-call preparation and rehearsal of roles is essential.

Summary driven, customer friendly features and benefits

For many years, the features and benefits of products and services have been the foundation of what sales teams are taught. Most of us have heard many times that customers buy benefits, not features. Many decision-makers are not as interested in how a product works as they are in how they will benefit from the product. In some cases, however, technically oriented buyers or decision-influencers are very interested in the features and how they work. As such, how we explain a product has a lot to do with the interests of the PCCRs and their perceptions of what is important.

Let's revisit the example of our salesperson with Ultra Matrix that is selling the real estate mutual fund to the financial advisor. From the discovery summary in the previous chapter, the important points we can tie into with our features and benefits would include:

- John, the financial advisor, has many clients who have too much money sitting in cash that is not increasing in value.
- He also has clients who are concerned about high stock market prices and are frustrated that they didn't get in when market prices were lower.
- He has clients who are more comfortable with real estate than stocks.
- He's concerned that the fees in real estate funds might be too high for his comfort level.

Now, let's look at a dull, plain, unpersonalized slice of a product presentation by our salesperson that touches on these needs in a generic way.

"Our new Metro Dynamics Commercial Real Estate Fund invests in commercial real estate to generate growth instead of income, which gives you a new option for your investors. The management team has deep expertise in finding commercial properties that can grow in value. In the past, only institutional investors with $25 million minimum to invest could get into these investments, but now that minimum has been reduced to just $35,000. We've created a more transparent way of showing fees, and with new share classes it's easier for retail investors to get involved. Our track record of mid-teens annual returns over the last twenty years is impressive and gives you confidence to recommend this new fund to your clients."

Now, let's look at a more effective example by a salesperson who uses customer-oriented phrasing and more attention to linking the discovery summary with better benefits.

"A lot of advisors we're working with are finding our Metro Dynamics Commercial Real Estate fund the perfect fit for many of their clients. You mentioned you have a number of clients who are sitting on too much cash. This fund is tailor-made for these clients. With its focus on growth and not on monthly income, advisors are recommending this fund and having real success getting money off the sidelines and into a fund with a twenty-year track record of annual returns in the mid-teens. Just like you, many advisors tell us that some of their clients are more familiar and comfortable with real estate than stocks. This fund invests in properties that generate great rental income and are easy to upgrade to increase property values, which is how we generate such consistent long-term results. Investors like how easy it is to buy this fund, its variety of share classes, and its $35,000 minimum. Unlike so many real estate REITS, it has a daily NAV so it can easily give them a reliable portfolio valuation. More importantly, advisors love the increased transparency and liquidity, which makes it easier to get out of the fund with far less liquidity concerns. Clients love the fact that there's no extended lockup on their capital. It's helping clients get money off the sidelines and into an investment that will grow steadily. It's a new tool to differentiate yourself from your competitors."

Here's an example of the digital ad agency and Barbara, the restaurant entrepreneur

Based on the discovery summary in the previous chapter with Barbara, the restaurant owner, we can link our features and benefits to the following points:

- Barbara feels comfortable with TV and radio, but her business is down and she's starting to realize she needs to change.
- She knows mobile is popular, but doesn't feel comfortable yet in this new digital area.
- She sees opportunity to grow during certain slow days and times.
- Barbara eventually wants to open three new restaurants.

A generic solution might sound like this:

> *"Barbara, with our partnership and mobile strategy, we'll be able to grow your business again. First of all, with an emphasis on mobile, you can target customers closest to your locations. And with custom messaging we can adapt your strategy to drive more traffic to you when you're slower, and we can adjust the actual message that different customers see. All in all, this will be key for you, especially as you consider opening new restaurants."*

A more compelling personalized version might include something like this:

> *"Barbara, top-tier restaurants that are growing in today's ultra-competitive market are committed to mobile solutions. It can feel intimidating to change, but it's our job to support you as a partner. The best restaurants have cracked the code on "the spontaneous diner" as you called them. With geo-targeting on mobile, we can work together to target these people who are closest to your restaurants, to drive traffic to you and take advantage of spontaneous impulses. And you mentioned that you want to be more consistent during your 'cold periods.' Forward thinking marketers get ahead of this with the custom and nimble messaging on mobile. In your case, we can increase the number of your customers on your slower days, Mondays and Thursdays, to drive extra traffic to you then. And more importantly, we can test and adjust your messaging so that people know about your lunch specials during lunch and your drink specials during happy hours. Finally, you said you will have 'made your mark' as a restaurant owner when you have opened three more restaurants to get to ten overall. As we test and learn at your existing locations, we'll be able to take those insights and apply them to your future launches so that you make a huge splash with each of your new openings over the next couple years."*

Three key elements make the latter version better:

- Customer-oriented phrasing, similar to what we learned in sales messaging
- Using PCCR feedback from the discovery summary to introduce product features
- Showing the PCCR how the features create relevant benefits for her

We've got some fantastic planning forms and features/benefits worksheets on competeselling.com to help you, but the process is fairly simple:

- Identify what opportunities you can address from the discovery summary and use the PCCR's own words to link your features/benefits to his or her needs.
- Identify a feature and explain how this feature will benefit the PCCR.
- Use a bridging statement to connect the feature to the benefit. A bridging statement is a short phrase, such as: What this does for you . . ." or "This is important for you, because . . ." (Notice that you should include the word "you.")
- Demonstrating the value of the benefit is absolutely critical. Your

presentation has to be compelling and desirable by solving a problem and/or addressing a need that the PCCR shared during discovery. The more you can use the PCCR's words to explain the way your solution solves the PCCR's needs, the better.

For practice, we suggest you review one of your recent sales interactions. Write out a short summary from the discovery step and then use the tools on competeselling.com to prepare a full customer-oriented, summary driven features and benefits presentation. The practice will help you understand how it all fits together. Our practice coaches at the SalesGym can also help you.

Blending ideas, solutions, features, and buying criteria insights

Compete Selling is about bringing NEW INSIGHTS into the conversation. Here is an example of how our mutual fund salesperson could introduce three insights in a three-by-three manner:

- Three-by-three headline: Real estate used for growth is often a good option.
    - Many investors are more comfortable with real estate than stocks, which is why more advisors are using real estate in more creative ways.
- Three-by-three headline: Today's high-priced equities are a good reason to consider adding more real estate to a portfolio.
    - Investors are sitting on cash because they're afraid the stock market is too volatile. They don't want to be suckers who bought at the top of the market, so they need more choices to achieve growth than what most advisors are recommending.
- Three-by-three headline: Too much money in cash gives your competitors an opening.
    - Many advisors realize that investors often have an overly conservative approach to investing, which results in poor returns. Therefore, investors are more easily convinced by competing advisors to try a better strategy. A growth strategy based on real estate can give you a competitive edge.

Here's how the digital marketing seller could position a three-by-three:

- Three-by-three headline: With mobile you can be hyper-local.
    - You can communicate to people on their phones when they're physically closest to your restaurants and most likely to visit.

- Three-by-three headline: Digital solutions can focus on intent.
  - When people are "searching" online for food or restaurants, they're actively looking, which means that mobile ads can be more effective than passive radio and TV ads that target unengaged audiences.
- Three-by-three headline: Digital communication is extremely dynamic.
  - We can continuously change your message based on the day of the week or the time of the day so that we can always communicate the most relevant, enticing information.

Insights are focused more on changing a way of thinking than pushing a product. It's important for you to organize your paradigm-breaking insights and to learn to communicate them in an interesting, engaging, and persuasive way. These insights should lead to tangible desirable results for your PCCR. It's often best to explain them in terms of how other customers are taking advantage of this new way of thinking to make it easier to understand.

Address likely objections in the solution step

We believe it is usually better to address likely objections early in the process. Nearly all of our SalesGym clients, before they start a project with us, find it hard to believe we can figure out their sales messaging and understand their business and sales process well enough to tailor our training and coaching sessions to their salespeople. The truth is, this is one of our strongest competitive advantages because we've done it so many times. But because many PCCRs have a hard time doing it, they assume it would be impossible for an outsider like us at the SalesGym to figure it out quickly. This can easily be addressed using the CPET process we learned back in chapter 3. Here's an example we might use when speaking with an interested prospect:

"Nearly all of our clients, before they start a project with us, ask us a common question: 'How can you understand our sales messaging and process so quickly when we have a hard time understanding it ourselves? Won't it take weeks of expensive consulting to figure it all out and tailor the solutions to our company?' (Here comes the CPET.) Let's be honest: That's a great question because sales messaging for a lot of business leaders is a challenge to understand, let alone teach to a sales team. What our top-performing customers tell us after we start a project is that we have an amazingly simple process that's not only effective, but transferable. They also like how we draw on our big archive of past projects to show them how similar companies made their sales messaging much better. They're relieved that the process of figuring out, refining, and recording fantastic sales messaging examples typically only takes two or three days of consulting time. They also realize, after they read a little about *Compete Selling*, that this process adapts to nearly all sales cycles and is often even better than what their salespeople are doing. It's this combination of expert sales messaging and an improved sales process that accelerates results. Some customers are still skeptical, but when they learn about our no-questions-asked guarantee, they're usually receptive to at least a small test. If I could ask you, how consistent are your salespeople when it comes to communicating your value proposition, differentiating factors, and competitive advantages?"

Here's a version used by our salesperson with Barbara, the restaurant owner:

"Our clients are often unsure when they first make a foray into digital. They ask us all the time, 'How will I know if digital will work for my business?' It's a reasonable question. After clients have experienced digital marketing for a few months, they tell us they are excited and that they are learning more about their ability to be agile and to measure results by simply observing their customers' experience. With digital, the ability to test and iterate is easy and fast. Our clients work with a dedicated digital analyst. They love that relationship because the analyst shows them exactly what specific messaging and strategies are working, so they can doubledown there. The analyst also shows them recommended changes that can be made in real time. Additionally, our retail clients who commit to mobile advertising start to see more consumers walking in to their locations while still looking at mobile ads and offers on their phones. So mobile and digital approaches provide flexibility, and the ability to measure and to see real results. So, in your case Barbara, how do you feel about the ability to measure your advertising efforts?"

Competitor vaccinations (raising the bar by emphasizing your strengths)

Vaccinating your competition is a great technique in the solution/presentation step of the process. We do this by drawing attention to the buying criteria that represent the weaknesses of our competitors.

For instance, the mutual fund salesperson's company's funds have a real advantage because all the fund managers invest at least $1 million of their own money in the funds they manage. Investors love this because they intuitively sense the manager will be more careful when their own money is on the line. Here's how a vaccination could work in this example.

"John, regardless of whether you use our funds, I would like to make a suggestion. I'd ask you to consider the wisdom of insisting that all the funds you recommend to your clients meet a simple, but extremely important standard. Insist that any fund you use is managed by a fund manager who has at least $1 million of their own money in it. Russ Kinnell, director of research for Morningstar, has repeatedly written about how important that one characteristic is to long-term fund performance. It's a great standard for the funds you use in the future. I'm curious about your thoughts on building a strategy around fund managers who have a stronger track record of protecting capital. Would that approach resonate with some of your overly conservative investors?"

End your competitor vaccination with a relevant open-ended question

After you've drawn attention to what you'd like your PCCR to pay more attention to, which correlates to your competitors' weaknesses, ask an open-ended question that is relevant to the point you just made. This is one of the important keys to reducing resistance. Questions need to be relevant to the flow of what has just been said.

Our digital salesperson knows that most competitors do not have simple reporting solutions. He knows they often have a "black box" (non-transparent) way of communicating about their fee placements. Here's an example of intentionally vaccinating the competitors with a thoughtful question.

"Barbara, as you work through the process of selecting a partner, I'd encourage you to ask yourself two questions: First, how easy is it to measure the results of your advertising dollars? Ask your agency contacts to show you a report of what your results look like and make sure it's easy to understand. Second, how transparent is your provider with where your dollars are going? If you invest $10 thousand per month, how much of that actually goes to the agency? This is a number you should know and feel good about. I'm curious, Barbara, how important is complete transparency about measurement and reporting to you as you invest in your future growth?"

An effective example we might use in the SalesGym could be, "Rick, regardless of whether you use the SalesGym to train your team in the future, one suggestion I'd make to you based on the nearly one hundred years of experience from our founding team is to ask every training organization that you consider working with what their plan is to ensure that every salesperson gets intense, weekly, one-on-one practice coaching over a period of at least three months. We know that solid practice is the most important element when it comes to retention, building new habits, and applying new skills. Ask them to tell you about their practice system and coaches. Our clients repeatedly tell us that putting more attention and money into follow-up practice coaching generates better results than live programs that offer no follow-up practice coaching. If I could ask you, what selling habits do you want your salespeople to build in the next six months that would accelerate new account acquisition?"

Evidence: internal and third-party (WSSBY = who says so besides you?)

Top performing salespeople are usually highly effective at finding and using evidence to back up their sales presentations. They have learned to use a wide variety of evidence and not to rely only on brochures and marketing pieces that come from their own company.

Consider that PCCRs are going to be at least somewhat skeptical of the information, statistics, and print pieces you provide from your company, and for good reason. That's why it's always a good idea to look for articles and published information by reliable, third-party sources that support your solution and recommendations.

For instance, our mutual fund salesperson needs to watch for articles about how real estate is essential to clients' portfolios from the *Wall Street Journal, Morningstar, Barrons, Forbes*, and other trustworthy investing publications.

Our digital ad salesperson must be alert to articles about the changing trends in advertising response, about how mobile is impacting consumer decisions in retail shopping, and about how the old rules of advertising have changed.

At the SalesGym, we're on the constant lookout for studies that show how important follow-up reinforcement and ongoing coaching and practice is to skill development and retention.

Be on the lookout for articles from reliable third-party sources to help reinforce the points you want to make. If a PCCR asks, "Who says so besides you?" then you can answer with credible third-party evidence.

Hidden costs and risks (impacting buying criteria)

In *The Challenger Sale*, many pages were devoted to the important topic of hidden costs and risks. People make decisions to attract positive results and to avoid negative results. For instance, some may choose certain diets in order to lose weight and to look better. Others may change their diet to avoid disease. Neither is better, just different.

Often, when a PCCR is comfortable with his or her current provider (your competitor) it isn't all that effective to point out a few benefits they could get by switching to you. It can be more motivating and startling to make the PCCR unavoidably aware of the hidden costs of their current choices and/or buying habits.

Here's an example of how our mutual fund salesperson applied this technique:

> *"An advisor I was working with a few weeks ago told me how frustrated he was that so many of his clients are sitting on too much cash. He's tried to get them back into the market, but as the market keeps going higher, his clients are even more convinced that they've missed out. So, they don't want to risk getting in at the top. Together, we did an analysis of his five highest net-worth clients who have had too much money on the sidelines over the last five years. We figured out that the clients had a combined $12 million in cash. Based on that amount, we discovered that they could have earned $4.5 million in returns if they had been in a conservatively managed equity fund. They could have earned $6.7 million if they had been in our real estate growth fund. That's why we need to take action now. Let's put together a presentation for these investors to make them aware of how costly their investing habits are and show them how commercial real estate can help solve their problems."*

Here's a version from our digital marketing seller.

> *"As I'm sure you see, today you're not only competing with other nice restaurants, you're competing with new channels. Home delivery isn't just pizza anymore. With mobile apps like DoorDash and UberEATS, people can order food from high-end restaurants and stay in their own homes. People are searching for food and inspiration on their mobile phones, so this is where we need to be. Whether they end up ordering from you for delivery, or whether they see an ad and consider coming in to the restaurant, this is the new marketplace where we need to have a strong presence in order to grow. You are currently missing out on this additional business, but we can fix that immediately."*

The key to this technique is to show the PCCR the costs of their decisions or lack of decisions and make it painful enough to get them to change. We've got some great worksheets online to help you work through this process.

Amplify your solution and ideas with technology

Technology is rapidly changing the way we sell and present ideas and information. On any given day, my schedule is filled with conference calls, video conferences, and meetings that involve robots. Recently, I was in a meeting where a small robot "walked" into the room and took a place at the conference table. Its face screen lit up, showing a man sitting in his home in Stockholm who attended our meeting just like he was in the room.

The key to technology is to make sure it works. Test it out. Rehearse. Practice and practice until it AMPLIFIES your message and doesn't distract. When technology glitches and hiccups surface in a sales presentation, the odds of making the sale start slipping. Far too many sales calls are ruined by technology that doesn't work smoothly. I sit in on conference calls every month during which the salesperson flubs their powerpoint presentation because they can't get their screen to share properly.

PRO TIP from Ross Robinson

> *One of the ways salespeople often kill momentum on a deal is by sending over a final proposal for their prospect to review hoping for a response only to hear nothing. Instead, leverage your proposal to get another meeting. Always set up a meeting with your prospect and let them know you're going to review and edit the proposal with them. People tend to support a world they help build. By positioning your meeting this way, you not only ensure that you keep the momentum of your deal going, but you also turn your meeting from a definite yes or no conversation into a discussion. It's much easier to answer questions and concerns in the moment with them, so use your proposal to ensure that happens.*

Some final thoughts on the solution presentation

As we said at the beginning of this chapter, we could easily fill a five-hundred-page book with all the thoughts, ideas, and examples of how to develop and deliver a solution presentation. However, very few people would read it which is why we gave you a short version of how to build better solutions.

This element of the sales process varies widely from one company to the next. For instance, in financial services, you may need a dozen highly technical analytic documents to present your data and analysis. In a tech company selling the latest whiz-bang artificial intelligence product, you may need a dazzling full-video demonstration. With other products, you may actually need the product to be in the room. Here is a quick summary of the universal elements that we believe are important for selling all products and services.

- Tap into the discovery summary repeatedly in the solution step.

- Use short headlines to set up key presentation points.
- Be creative with your evidence and bring some WSSBY into the room.
- Use customer-oriented phrasing throughout.
- Make sure your technology setup is bulletproof.
- Draw attention to your strengths and to your competitors' weaknesses by using competitor vaccination techniques.
- Address head-on the PCCR's likely objections and perceptions about your weaknesses.
- Make your PCCRs aware of the hidden costs and risks of their current thinking and decision making criteria.
- Test for interest, engagement, and reaction throughout.
- Focus on buying criteria as much as you focus on the product.
- Talk about how your best customers think about your products and services.
- Use stories, analogies, examples, and illustrations to make your claims simple and memorable.

Remember, the solution step of the process will only be as good as your discovery step. *Compete Selling* works better than consultative selling alone because it enables you to be far more assertive in the right way during discovery. This will uncover the concerns and objections EARLY, before you present your ideas, solutions, and proposals. This method will reduce the objections later in the process. In other words, if you don't ask better, more assertive questions, your solutions will often miss the mark.

Finally, PRACTICE is the key to getting better at this critically important element of selling. Set aside time each week to rehearse, record, and listen to how you present your most important key points. Record a three-by-three of your competitive advantages and listen to it. Set up practice sessions with another person on your team. If you want to practice with a demanding practice coach, talk to us at the SalesGym. If you don't practice consistently, you will never discover your full potential.

Nine

Responding to Concerns / Gaining Commitment

One of the smartest people I ever met in sales was also my first sales manager and boss. She told me early in my career that when you walk into a sales call, any sales call, whether you're ready to close or just starting the process, you should know what you'll be asking for at the end of the meeting. She added that you should always have at least two options for closing recommendations.

- The first, is a big idea, a stretch outcome that would represent either a big step forward or a big commitment to an order.
- The second should be a fallback offer, something smaller and perhaps more realistic, an option that is easy for the PCCR to say yes to.

She continued to explain that if you're really good, you learn how to present even big, stretch recommendations in a way that is easy to say yes to. Her final thought was that the cardinal sin in selling was to end a sales call with no recommendation at all. You don't want a call to end with: "I'll get back to you after you've had a week to think about it." Thud.

At the time she taught me this, I was early in my learning curve and had no idea how wise this advice was. Over the years, I've met and interviewed a lot of top performers, and when I'd ask them questions about closing, nearly all of them would say things like this:

- You've got to ask for the order in creative ways and make it easy to say yes and hard to say no. Make all the risks of a no clear and compelling.
- Make whatever next step you're recommending seem easy or less threatening.
- Never close a meeting without asking for at least some commitment to a next step in the process. You'll never know where you stand if you don't ask for commitment.
- Sometimes, you've got to ask for something small at first in order to get something big in the end. For a lot of salespeople, the process is longer and more complicated, but EVERY sales call needs to end with forward progress.
- If you're getting a lot of resistance in the closing step, it's probably because you didn't ask enough good, assertive questions earlier in the process.
- If you hear "maybe" and "I'll get back to you" too often, you probably need to make some changes to avoid clogging up your time-management system. Often, a NO is better than a maybe. Suggesting assertive next steps will help you get to yes or no and reduce your need to follow up with PCCRs that never pan out.

Let's go over some important things you can do to become better at closing, and to gain commitments to your recommendations.

- A good way to improve your closing skills is to become comfortable asking this question: What are the issues or concerns that need to be addressed before you'd feel good about looking at some options for our next steps?
- It's important to make a master list of stretch and fallback outcomes that you'd like to ask during and at the end of the sales process. This is especially true if a sale involves multiple calls or steps. Remember that fallback options are relatively low-risk recommendations that are easy for the PCCR to say yes to.
- Next, we need to identify customers who have made the decisions that lead to the stretch and fallback outcomes you identify. It will be helpful to know why they made the decision and how they benefited.

You can work all of this out by using the process worksheets on competeselling.com. So, let's address one of the best ways to set up a recommendation and to ask for action. It's called a customer success story.

Customer success stories are perfect to set up a next-step recommendation

Numerous books present different approaches for setting up next-steps and recommendations, but from our experience, there is no better way to advance a sale or to ask for the order than by using a customer success story. It is the most comfortable and easiest way to ask for the order, which is why, if you are good at it, it works so well. It feels much less threatening than blunt methods. Let's take a look at two examples. First, here's an example from our mutual fund salesperson:

"John, one advisor who reminds me of you had set a goal to try a new strategy with three of his clients who all had portfolios with way too much money on the sidelines. He worked with me to put together a client analysis to show how their portfolios would have performed over the last five years if they had placed their cash allocations in equities and in our Metro Dynamics Real Estate Growth Fund. I did a lot of the work, so it wasn't too difficult for him. Then, he set up a meeting when I was in town and we presented the reports. We also introduced the real estate growth fund as an alternative to what they believed was an overly volatile stock market. Instead of fighting a losing battle to convince them to move cash into the stock market, we tried a real estate strategy. The bad news is, all three of them did not take his recommendation; but, two of them moved a total of $3.5 million out of cash. Those clients really liked the real estate approach. Their investments are growing. Moveover, John has set himself above other advisors by having more options for market skeptics. I'd suggest we do the exact same thing with three of your investors and see what happens. Who do you think would be a good fit for this strategy?"

For our restaurant example:

"Barbara, I think you know we work with Max's, the high-end steakhouses. They have twenty locations around the Bay Area. Like you, they've relied on traditional media and a strong loyal customer base for years. But a year ago, they came to us and said that the number of customer visits at almost all of their locations was flat or down year-over-year. Their CEO, Max Milton, was smart to take action quickly. He took 40 percent of the ad money he had been investing in TV and committed that to a combination of search, mobile, and online video. He and his staff have a monthly call with an analyst to monitor, keep score, and make the right adjustments. In less than six months, traffic and sales have been so strong that Max now plans to open five more locations this year, and he has been moving more and more of his ad budget each month to his digital strategy. So, in your case, I'd suggest we start with 20 percent of your current TV and radio budget and invest that in a ninety-day intense strategy for three of your locations. We'll have real data that'll help us compare your online results with your traditional approaches. Does this make sense?"

Here's how we might use this approach in the SalesGym

"Bill, it probably seems like a big decision to determine whether our practice coaching system would be a good fit for your five hundred salespeople spread all over the country. A sales executive from a large tech firm who reminds me of you comes to mind because he wanted to test if our training and coaching approach would work for his team, but he was skeptical that we could tailor it to the degree he thought necessary. So, he picked only fifteen salespeople to try it out for three months. We agreed to give these fifteen people weekly practice sessions, a full effort with an honest evaluation. He helped us set up some meetings with ten top performers to refine their sales messaging and we did a short kickoff video conference event. Then we did the thirty-minute one-on-one practice coaching sessions by phone every week for three months, working through the entire sales process. We recorded every session and sent the recordings to their managers to evaluate. We tracked their sales over the three months so they could evaluate not only what was happening qualitatively, but also quantitatively. It was a low-risk, affordable way to find out if this radically different approach to rigorous sales coaching would work. I'd suggest that we do the same thing with your sales team. Let's identify ten to fifteen salespeople and try the process with them. You'll see exactly how we learn your sales messaging and sales process. You'll be able to hear, on the recordings and evaluations, how your people respond. What would be the best way to identify who would be a good fit for this test? Who should we talk to in order to get it figured out?"

Let's break down the steps of a closing recommendation customer success story

- We start with customer-oriented language, introducing a customer who faced a similar problem.
- We identify the problem or need that customer had.
- We explain the action they took or decision(s) they made.
- We explain the benefits that the customer got from that decision.
- We ask the PCCR to make the same decision in a non-threatening way that's EASY to say YES to (E2SY2).

We're not going to spend a lot of time in this book talking about other closing techniques that have been covered *ad nauseam* in other books such as: The Alternate Close; The Columbo Close; The Ben Franklin Close; The Assumptive Close; The Puppy Dog Close; The Backwards Close; The Hard Close; The Relationship Close; The Take Away Close. It's easy to find descriptions of these approaches with a simple search, but the success story approach, for whatever reason, hasn't received much attention in books. From our experience, it's by far the best. It does require, however, some extra preparation because you have to work out the details of success stories that fit the various recommendations that move toward your stretch and fallback outcomes.

Closing is tying up loose ends and summarizing too

We've found that top-performing salespeople are typically good with the communication that happens between meetings. Whether it's getting an agenda out before the meeting, or a thank you and summary after the meeting, closing has a lot to do with nailing down details and following up on them quickly. If you sell something that involves multiple steps, meetings, or conversations, then the power of a summary between those conversations cannot be overstated.

For example, here's a sample of a summary in the form of an email:

Hi John,

Thanks again for setting up our meeting yesterday. It was great figuring out an approach with you to present some ideas for helping your clients move money off the sidelines so that they can generate better returns. Just to recap our next steps, here's what I took away from the meeting:

- *I'm going to connect with your account manager, Julie, to talk with her about the three clients you have in mind for our real estate fund.*

- *We will work together to develop a simple analysis of the returns they could have achieved over the last five years had they invested in our suggested funds. I can have that ready by Monday, June 7.*

- *I'm coming back to see you on Thursday, June 10, and you're going to set up either in-person meetings in your office or phone appointments so that we can explain together how this real estate approach to growth works.*

- *I'll get you some fact sheets about the fund by tomorrow so that you can go over those with your team.*

If there are any details I missed, please let me know and I'll send you a quick update after I connect with Julie to confirm we've got it all on track. Thanks again for the opportunity to work with your clients. I'll be in touch in a few days.

Looking forward to helping you with your clients!

John Smith / Account Executive / Metro Dynamics Real Estate Growth Funds

Here's another follow up email to Barbara, the restaurant owner:

Barbara,

Thank you for making the time to meet today, and for letting me try your new take on gourmet chicken fingers. Delicious! So that we can maintain momentum and make fast progress together, here are the next steps we discussed:

- *Please email me contact info for Jeff, your marketing manager, and I'll connect him to Carolyn, our top digital analyst, so she can familiarize him with our reporting.*

• On Wednesday, I'll send you three mobile videos from successful retail and restaurant clients, so you can start thinking of ideas.

• Please send me a list of your most popular menu items and we can begin to work on online ad copy that drives traffic.

I appreciate your willingness to consider these new solutions and look forward to making progress together.

Thank you,

Brian Lewis/Account Executive

Tie down those follow-up steps in writing and do it professionally

You've got to tie down the important details with a professional summary that looks well-organized, is professionally written, and easy to follow. This projects competence and makes it much more likely that the follow-up steps will get done. It's been said many times that commitments are EASY to make, it's the follow-up that's hard. An ancient Chinese proverb also states:

"The faintest ink is more reliable than the best memory."

PRO TIP from Adam Shaivitz

I have a client named Shad and we meet about once a quarter in person, usually over lunch. We get along well and work on several projects together, and of course I'm always trying to be proactive and provide the next supportive solution. Almost all of my meetings with Shad end quickly, with him getting a text from his assistant or seeing a note that reminds him he has to run quickly to his next meeting.

When I'm not on my game, my parting comment is usually something like: "Thanks again for making time for lunch. I'll be sure to follow up." When I'm the best version of myself and I've prepared a couple of likely next steps (before the meeting ever began), I say something like: "Thanks again for making time for lunch. I'll send you a draft plan for you to edit and forward to Eric before next week."

Of course, I don't know exactly how my lunch meeting will go (before I get there). But I have a pretty good idea of two or three likely next steps I'll suggest at the end of the meeting. When I identify them in advance, I'm able to suggest them quickly and with more confidence and specificity when the time is tight.

People often ask, How do top sellers accelerate sales cycles? We all are in many meetings each day. When meetings end with specific next actions (like in the second example above) deals happen in weeks vs. months.

What about tough objections?

Inevitably, people ask what to do when their efforts don't work and a really tough objection gets in the way of the sale? We didn't spend a lot of time on what to do when this happens because it really depends on the situation. But here are a few thoughts.

- First, selling is hard and competitive; that's why it typically pays well. Nothing works 100 percent all of the time. Even the best sales professionals don't succeed on every call. That goes with the territory. Sometimes your product or service is simply not as good a fit or match as your competitor's.
- Remember, objections have more to do with buying criteria, biases, and beliefs than anything else. When you change the buyer's thinking about their buying criteria, you radically change their perception of objections.
- *Compete Selling* is about identifying the objections, barriers, and likely challenges EARLY in the sales process. We bring them up in our questioning and try to make the PCCR more comfortable talking about concerns before we present our product solutions.
- When big objections come up late in the process, after our solution presentation, it's often too late to overcome them. This doesn't mean we shouldn't be persistent, but it's one reason why relationship building consultative sellers are generating worse results than those who use the *Compete Selling* model.
- To respond to objections, just step back and use the process. We generally have to drop back to discovery, then offer a quick summary of the issue, then provide some more solution ideas along with evidence to overcome the objections, and another E2SY2 recommendation. Ideally, though, you should already have done this.
- If you are getting a lot of objections you can't overcome, you usually need more PRACTICE to get better at the earlier stages of the call.

The best HASPs at closing nearly always have these six advantages over their competitors:

- They build rapport better and faster, and they engender more trust.
- They have a way of asking assertive questions and creating a higher level of comfort so the PCCR will answer honestly without feeling threatened.

- Their solution presentation is more creative, and works on two levels:
    - A strong emphasis on impacting buying criteria and the THINKING of the PCCR to line-up better with their competitive advantages
    - Answering the question, "Who says so besides you?" in a balanced and compelling way
- They are far more effective at presenting the RISKS of not changing. They put a new perspective into the conversation that represents a better choice and makes the cost of not changing a real factor that is impossible to ignore.
- They have a much better sense of what recommendation will move the sale forward as quickly as possible, and they also make it easy for the customer to say yes.
- They practice more. They're highly prepared for all phases of the sales process.

PRO TIP from Mark Woodland

Don't play "Whack-a-Mole' with your prospects! Have you ever been to a place like Chucky Cheese? . . . You'll most likely find a simple game, where a kid with a hammer tries to whack the mole that pops up. As soon as the child swings the hammer the mole disappears and pops up in a different hole and the child tries to hit that one. You'd think that salespeople would be infinitely smarter than a six-year-old, but my experience is that when it comes to addressing concerns, we all too often act like that chubby kid with pizza on his face swinging the hammer. Rather than jump on the first concern out of the customer's mouth and trying to fix it, take a moment and ask a question or two, lower their resistance, make sure it's the right problem to address, and THEN respond.

Ten

The Compete Selling Amplifiers

We promised you on the first page of *Compete Selling* a short, contemporary, easy read on selling. There are lots of additional resources at competeselling.com to help you develop all the tools and skills covered in our blend of consultative and assertive HASP sales approaches. This is truly the "how to" manual of assertive selling while still winning friends and influencing people. It's easy to be aggressive, but it's difficult to be aggressive in a way that builds strong and trusting relationships. If our assertiveness is in the best interest of our PCCRs, they'll see us as more than a person pushing a product or service; they'll see us as people with better, more helpful ideas and thinking than our competitors. We need to be assertive in the right way, which is about helping our PCCRs see new ideas, choices, and decisions that will help them, their employees, and THEIR customers. It's not about more pressure during the close; it's about bringing new insights, game changing ideas, and the inspiration to make bolder and better decisions.

Let's close by drawing some attention to other skills, the intangibles that amplify results. Top-performing sales professionals have these skills. Although we're not going to spend a lot of time on them, trust us when we tell you it's important. We'll take them one-by-one and start with goals:

Goals are critically important and you have to write them down

What are your sales and activity goals this week, month, quarter, and year? Do you have them written down? Are they updated? If not, why not? Go to the competeselling.com goal development exercise immediately if you didn't answer yes to all of these questions.

Are you a fantastic communicator?

Sales has a lot to do with communication. You need to constantly hone your skills. Read books about communication, take public speaking courses, and learn to communicate better each month. Learn to tell better stories, and learn a few quotes and statistics that are relevant to what you sell. Another book we wrote, *If You're Not Out Selling, You're Being Out Sold*, goes into depth on how to improve your communications skills. Dale Carnegie's *How To Win Friends and Influence People* is an absolute classic and a must-read on this topic, too.

Get and stay motivated

Nothing feels better than waking up motivated and excited to get on with the day, to go after your goals, and nothing feels worse than struggling to find motivation to do even the easy stuff. Here are some well-tested tips to get and stay motivated.

- Review your goals frequently (every week). Write them down and keep track of your progress in a simple goal journal.
- Spend more time with successful people and limit your time with complainers, negative people, and excuse blamers. Successful, motivated people will help you get and stay motivated.
- Read good, motivational stuff frequently. Avoid news and sources that give you lots of negative things to think about that you have virtually no ability to influence.
- Realize that health and VITALITY is the greatest treasure in life. Get in shape. Exercise and keep your body moving. Being in a body that feels great and has strength, stamina, and flexibility will help you have the energy to out sell your competition. It is one of the great luxuries in life most of us can obtain if we get serious about it. Your brain power is intimately connected to your level of fitness and vitality. It will think better, faster, and with more processing power if your body feels better and has more energy. You'll be driving more watts into the processor!
- Waste less time. Limit how much time you put into addictive, non-productive activities. Don't do that stuff while you're working. Create results, achieve your vision, and minimize distractions.
- Spend less time trying to figure out what went wrong and whose fault it was, and instead figure out how to improve the situation. Then do it. Too much time spent placing blame is one of the biggest mistakes when it comes to building relationships.
- Remember the ten two-letter words that can change your life:

If it is to be, it is up to me!

You are the master of your life and fate. It takes just as much time to be wildly successful as it does to be mediocre. The effort to be motivated, healthy, filled with vitality, and successful is worth it. Go for it. Get in charge of the decisions and habits you need to break and form.

Interpersonal skills are essential too

We can build relationships with natural curiosity and interest in others, by listening and using problem-solving skills. Generally speaking, decision-makers usually choose to do business with people they trust and like to be around. A high percentage of top-performing salespeople and executives we've met over the years are remarkably effective at building relationships. They are interesting to be around because they ask good questions, listen, and can get things done without aggravating the people around them.

Believe it or not, in this short little book ...

We've covered a lot of ground. It was our intention to quickly share a lot of new ideas that have been tested and refined in the SalesGym. Competeselling.com is a great online resource to help you go deeper, with worksheets and process guides. Let's take a quick review of all the key areas we covered:

- The factors that make highly assertive sales professionals (HASPs) different
- How to focus on opportunity limiting biases and beliefs of PCCRs before selling products and services
- Merging consultative and higher assertiveness selling
- Creating useful competitive advantages headlines
- Customer-oriented phrasing
- The CPET process
- The three-by-three technique
- Credibility statements
- A practical pre-call planning checklist
- The essential consultative selling questioning flow
- Using conventional and contrasting thinking to set up assertive questions
- Using customer-oriented observations to set up better questions
- "A question I often get . . ." tee-up of a HASP question or likely objection
- How to use a better discovery summary
- How to take better notes leading to better summaries
- Summary driven features and benefits that resonate
- Using third-party evidence to get to "Who says so besides you" (WSSBY)
- Competitor vaccinations to impact buying criteria
- The importance of moving likely objections up in the sales process
- Planning with stretch and fallback outcomes
- Using effective success stories for closing recommendations
- E2SY2 recommendations
- Tying down follow-up details

There are many other longer, very good books on consultative selling, and the challenger books do a great job of presenting some compelling research; but this is the only book we know of that provides you with the entire package of **how** to do it.

Think for a moment about great athletes

Day after day for years, starting when they were young, they practiced, worked out, and steadily improved. They spent a lot more time practicing with coaches than actually competing.

We've found in working with thousands of sales professionals over the last twenty-five years that verbal selling skills, or what we call "sales fluency," is acquired in a similar way that athletic skills are built: through effective practice, developing the right techniques, and working with an experienced coach who can demonstrate what "great" really looks like.

For most salespeople who are generating average results, the most important missing factor is the lack of a steady, weekly practice routine using a proven approach to break bad habits, build good ones, and IMPROVE. There is no substitute for practice. Knowledge is not enough. Knowing what to do will only get you so far. It's the ability to perform under pressure that makes all the difference. Any mediocre golfer knows they need to hit the ball solid and straight; they have that knowledge, but the knowledge DOES NOT translate into skill without repetition and practice. Performing well under pressure takes practice. There's a true miracle to discover with steady, weekly practice. It significantly improves skills, attitude, motivation, and the odds of success. Practicing with a strong coach will greatly improve your results.

Practice **DOES NOT** make perfect.
Practice makes **PERMANENT**.

PERFECT PRACTICE makes perfect.
Practice **WITH A SKILLED COACH** = perfect practice.

In closing, get a great practice partner or coach and practice more, set goals, get in shape, commit to a serious sales skills practice routine, become a great communicator, and become a JEDI level master of *Compete Selling* so you generate better results in less time and literally hold all the keys to your career destiny.

It's been our pleasure to share our insights with you. We are grateful to all our clients we get to work with and learn from every day in the SalesGym. We look forward to and welcome the opportunity to practice with you someday and we'd like to leave you with a final thought from the good folks in Ireland.

The Irish Prayer

May the road rise up to meet you.
May the wind be always at your back.
May the sun shine warm upon your face;
the rains fall soft upon your fields
and until we meet again,
May grace and good fortune surround you
and all of those you love.

Notes

Made in the USA
Columbia, SC
13 April 2018